ASTD's Ultimate Train-the-Trainer: A Complete Guide to Training Success

ASTD Ultimate Series

ELAINE BIECH

ASTD
PRESS

Alexandria, Virginia

ASTD Press is an internationally renowned source of insightful and practical information on workplace learning and performance topics, including training basics, evaluation and return on investment, instructional systems development, e-learning, leadership, and career development.

Ordering information: Books published by ASTD Press can be purchased by visiting ASTD's website at store.astd.org or by calling 800.628.2783 or 703.683.8100.

Library of Congress Control Number: 2008937406

ISBN-10: 1-56286-587-0
ISBN-13: 978-1-56286-587-0

ASTD Press Editorial Staff:
Director: Dean Smith
Manager, Acquisitions and Author Relations: Mark Morrow
Editorial Manager: Jacqueline Edlund-Braun
Senior Associate Editor: Tora Estep
Editorial Assistant: Georgina Del Priore
Full-Service Design, Editing, and Production: Aptara Inc., Falls Church, VA, www.aptaracorp.com
    Development/Production Editor: Robin C. Bonner
    Copyeditor: Ellen N. Feinstein
    Indexer: Kidd Indexing
    Proofreader: Sarah A. Bonner
    Interior Design: Lisa Adamitis
Cover Design: Rose McLeod
Cover Illustration: Shutterstock.com

Printed by Versa Press, Inc., East Peoria, Illinois, www.versapress.com

For Shane and Thad
The Ultimate Kids

The ASTD Ultimate Series

ASTD Press's *Ultimate* series is a natural follow-on to the popular *Trainer's WorkShop* series. Like the *Trainer's WorkShop* series, the *Ultimate* series is designed to be a one-stop, practical, hands-on road map that helps you quickly develop training programs. Each book in the *Ultimate* series offers a full range of practical tools you can apply or adapt to a variety of training scenarios. As in the *Trainer's WorkShop* series, you will find exercises, handouts, assessments, structured experiences, and ready-to-use presentations, along with detailed facilitation instructions. So what's the difference? The *Ultimate* series aims to present the full scope of various topics, offering today's overcommitted training professionals even MORE practical and scalable help: More practical exercises, handouts, assessments, and other ready-to-deploy training solutions. More detailed instructions. Broader topic coverage. More downloadable material. In short, more value for your training budget dollars.

Contents

Acknowledgments

ASTD's Ultimate Train-the-Trainer: A Complete Guide to Training Success was written with verbal and written advice from many professionals. I have learned more than you can know from the professional examples of others who continue to teach me: Jean Barbazette, Geoff Bellman, Ken and Margie Blanchard, Peter Block, Ann Herrmann-Nehdi, Don Kirkpatrick, Jim Kouzes, Jack and Patti Phillips, Bob Pike, Dana and Jim Robinson, Pam Schmidt, Mel Silberman, Thiagi, and Jack Zenger. I am in awe of all of you.

A special thank-you to
- Mark Morrow, editor, for one more exciting challenge
- Cat Russo, publisher, for trusting that I could meet the needs of ASTD and the profession
- Dean Smith, Jacqueline Edlund-Braun, Tora Estep, and Georgina Del Priore, ASTD editorial staff, for another great opportunity
- Robin Bonner for your dedicated, comprehensive professionalism and for making me look good with your editing prowess
- Lorraine Kohart, the newest consultant on the block
- Dan Greene, for being a sport and taking me to funny movies
- My clients, for allowing me to experiment with you, especially the Office of Naval Research and its talent manager, Will Brown.

Elaine Biech
ebb associates inc
Norfolk, VA

Preface

Introduction to ASTD's Ultimate Train-the-Trainer

Training is the ultimate profession. Training touches everyone at every age, in every occupation, in all walks of life, throughout the world. Training opens doors to additional opportunities, opens eyes to innovative ideas, and opens minds to fresh concepts.

Training can resolve problems, prepare the unqualified, guide those who need direction, and give hope to those who are desperate. Training encourages, excites, enables, enriches, enlightens, and empowers. Being a trainer is the ultimate job if you want to make a difference in the world.

Preparing others for this profession by conducting a train-the-trainer is the ultimate assignment. Conducting a train-the-trainer session is an honor. It signifies that you have reached a certain level of expertise: You have the skills and knowledge and you have enough experience under your belt to be recognized as the ultimate trainer—someone who assists others in learning the craft.

So what advice do you give a competent individual, like yourself, who is in the ultimate profession with the ultimate assignment? Two things:

- Maintain your spark.
- Light fires.

Maintain Your Spark

To stay effective as a trainer, you must maintain the spark of excitement that demonstrates that you love what you do. If you are conducting train-the-trainer sessions, you are most likely one of those trainers who does not get up to "go to work" in the morning but instead gets up to "go play." Even so, maintaining your excitement may be difficult at times if you are repeatedly conducting the same learning experience. Perhaps these suggestions will help you.

Become a life-long learner. The life-long learner concept is not new, but finding new ways to learn is. Attending a virtual learning event, taking a class at your local college, attending the ASTD International Conference & Exposition, learning a new computer program, or reading the latest business books are all good suggestions. But have you thought of leisure outings as learning experiences? Go fishing with your significant other. Visit a museum with your children, grandchildren, or the kid next door. Take lessons in a new sport. Purchase and read a magazine you've *never* read before. Peruse a different book section at your bookstore. Visit a toy store and play as if you were seven years old. At work, you can get yourself a mentor. Or, learn more about your organization by shadowing a manager who works in a department about which you know little. All of these experiences will add breadth to your knowledge base and excitement to your discussions. And think of the stories they will spawn when you are conducting training!

Expand your network. Networking is one of the best ways to maintain your spark. Meeting others and getting their perspectives produces new ways for you to approach life. Professional organizations can provide a networking list of people you can contact. The next time you attend a local ASTD chapter meeting, schedule lunch with another attendee. Every person you meet ignites new ideas for how you approach life and your work as a trainer.

Become the best. Your participants expect you to be on the leading edge of advances in the field. Establish standards for yourself that will keep you on your training toes, reaching ever higher for the bar of excellence. List your training values and what you believe in as a trainer. Obtain certification or accreditation in your chosen field: a Certified Professional in Learning and Performance (CPLP) as a trainer, a Certified Speaking Professional (CSP) as a speaker, a Certified Professional Facilitator (CPF) as a facilitator, or whatever is most relevant. What you learn becomes the kindling to feed the flames of excitement as you deliver your next training session.

Try something new. Find ways to make every training session as exciting as your first, by incorporating new activities, doing something different (like serving popcorn with a movie), inviting guest speakers, or co-facilitating with a colleague. Trying something new in a training session keeps the training fresh for both you and your participants. Make it a dynamite training session!

Light Fires

The most rewarding aspect of my career occurs when former participants tell me that something I said in a session inspired them to make a significant change in their lives. As a trainer, you inspire others to use their talents and expand their horizons. You encourage them to try something new. You excite them with possibilities. You energize them about their work. And you renew their confidence in themselves and their value to their employer.

Model excellence. To inspire, encourage, excite, energize, and renew, you need to model what you expect your participants to do. When you conduct a train-the-trainer session, your participants will look at your presentation as the "correct way" to conduct training. Of course you will not do everything perfectly. When you do err, though, use it as a learning moment. Be honest about what happened and open the incident up to discussion. You will be respected even more for being honest and candid.

Stay ahead of trends. Everybody's talking about them. Whether it's a discussion about how the Obama campaign was run or a dialogue on how the building industry can become "green," trends are the focal point of many conversations. A few of the trends that have an effect on the training profession include social networking, multi-tasking and partial attention, accessibility, high levels of stress, super-sizing and fast pacing, and customizing for globalization. Demonstrating new concepts as a trainer requires you to stay ahead of the trends.

Make yourself available. Your participants will look to you as the "go to" person for almost anything: book referrals, help in finding resources, introductions, or just a willing ear. Whatever the reason, make time and make space in your busy life to assist in whatever way you can. Addressing participants' requests may not be in your job description, but this task is critical to being a professional who makes a difference in the world.

Be prepared to coach. This is related to making yourself available. Participants will come to you asking for advice. Sometimes you will have some ideas, and other times you may not. Usually, they will have the answers inside them and you will just need to guide them through a series of questions to help them discover those answers. Learn a few coaching skills to keep the fires of knowledge burning that you lit while your participants were in your training session.

Be the Best of the Best

The book you hold in your hands provides you with the basics for providing the "ultimate" experience for your participants. To be the best of the best, however, requires investment on your part—an investment in *you*. What better place to invest?

Find ways to maintain your spark: Become a life-long learner, expand your network, become the best, and try something new.

Gear up to light fires: Model excellence, stay ahead of trends, make yourself available, and be prepared to coach.

As the ultimate trainer in the ultimate profession delivering the ultimate assignment you have the capacity to create spontaneous combustion. Maintain your spark as a trainer. Light a fire of desire in each of your participants.

Elaine Biech
Norfolk, VA
July 2009

Finding Your Way Around: How to Use This Book Effectively   1

What's in This Chapter?

- An overview of the entire book

- Ways in which this book will support you in conducting a train-the-trainer workshop

- Descriptions of what the icons represent

- Descriptions of the contents of the CD

- Introduction to the jargon used throughout the book

▲   ▲   ▲

Train-the-Trainer: A Blessing or a Curse?

A train-the-trainer workshop is the most unique training you can deliver. It is a metatraining, that is, you are actively modeling exactly the same thing that you are training your participants to do (*meta* being a prefix meaning "within" or "among")! This can be either a blessing or a curse.

A train-the-trainer session is a blessing because you can easily take advantage of the setting. You don't have to make up case studies—the session *is* a case study. You don't have to create role plays—you are playing the role right in front of your participants' eyes. You don't have to go on a field trip—you are in the middle of the action. However...

A train-the-trainer session is a curse because you are modeling the very skills you are explaining. You are "on" 100 percent of the time. You can bet participants are watching what you are doing. They're wondering if you do what you tell them to do. To quote a tired old phrase, "Do you walk the talk?" So, what happens when you are not the perfect model? Take advantage of imperfection by turning it into a lesson. When things go wrong, turn it into an opportunity for participants to problem solve what they will do when the same thing happens to them.

Sometimes modeling can backfire. Once, the fire alarm rang as I was speaking at a conference. I was presenting "creativity," and the participants refused to leave the room because they thought that I had planted the alarm as part of my "creative" demonstration!

Although you have to be better prepared for conducting a train-the-trainer workshop than almost any other training you will ever conduct, it is an honor to have a chance to share your knowledge and expertise with your colleagues.

Train-the-Trainer Content

The content of this book aligns with the ADDIE model. ADDIE is the commonly accepted instructional systems design (ISD) training cycle used by most people in the workplace learning and performance (WLP) profession; it represents the process used to create and deliver training. The acronym stands for *a*nalysis, *d*esign, *d*evelopment, *i*mplementation, and *e*valuation. The three-day train-the-trainer session, which covers all the train-the-trainer content in this book, is divided into five modules:

1. **Module 1—Introduction:** the welcome, objectives, and introduction to the content.

2. **Module 2—Assess and Analyze:** the importance of assessing learners' needs and ways to gather data.

3. **Module 3—Design and Develop:** how a training designer, using the data gathered in the needs assessment, creates learning objectives. These objectives provide the foundation for creating a training program to help adult learners gain the required skills and knowledge.

4. **Module 4—Implement and Facilitate:** how to facilitate the training session confidently and competently, while keeping the focus on the learner.

5. **Module 5—Evaluate and Enhance:** the importance of evaluation, Kirkpatrick's four levels of evaluation, and the need to use what you learn from evaluation to make improvements.

To make it easy for you, the same numbers are used to identify the teaching materials and the modules in the Trainer's Guide (chapters 5 through 9). Each of the participant handouts has a number and a title at the top of the first page. (Most handouts are only one page in length, but a few are longer.) The number refers to the module, as well as the number of the handout within the module. For example, **handout 3-13**, Know Your Training Style, is the 13th handout in module 3, Design and Develop. It's referenced in chapter 7, "Trainer's Guide: Module 3—Design and Develop."

Training Basics: Adults and Learning

The title of this book is *ASTD's Ultimate Train-the-Trainer: A Complete Guide to Training Success*. I chose the subtitle with great care. Although *A Complete Guide to Training Success* refers to your success in conducting the session, focusing on the success of your participants is even more important. As a competent and credible trainer, you are responsible for making sure that your focal point is to address your participants' needs. As Stolovitch and Keeps say in *Telling Ain't Training*, "Start with the learner and never lose focus" (Stolovitch and Keeps, 2002).

Focusing on the success of your learners is even more important in a train-the-trainer session. You are going to train adults who will train other adults. (There's that meta thing going on again.) Adults bring to the table these attributes:

- They have a great deal of experience, and they should be encouraged to share their knowledge and skills.
- They have responsibilities, and they may think they have more important things to do than attend your training event.
- They strongly need to know why they should learn something and how it will help them cope with daily life.
- They harbor images of themselves as self-directing individuals who desire control of what they do.

A version of these concepts was first presented by Malcolm Knowles in his book, *The Adult Learner: A Neglected Species,* published in 1973. The wise trainer incorporates these concepts into any training that is designed or delivered. As the trainer, you will be successful if you are able to do these things:

- create a safe learning environment
- ensure that your content is transferable and solves participants' problems
- encourage participation
- treat your participants with respect and value their ideas
- prepare for any situation, so that you can easily meet all participants' needs.

Support Within These Two Covers

Each chapter has been designed mostly as a stand-alone discussion, so if you are an experienced trainer who needs good material to conduct a train-the-trainer session immediately, you can go straight to chapter 11, to see what we offer in the way of participant material.

The book is designed with you in mind. The initial premise of the book is that you have a group of individuals who need a complete train-the-trainer session that encompasses all of the steps in the ADDIE model. Alternative support emanates from that premise. For example, if you only need to provide information about data collection, writing learning objectives, or establishing a positive learning environment, you can just select the activities related to each specific topic.

The book provides all of the participant materials (called handouts, which are provided on the CD and in thumbnail form in chapter 11), the PowerPoint slides, and the Trainer's Guide to support the delivery of the three-day train-the-trainer or shorter sessions that you may require.

The book also includes support to you as a trainer, so you can plan and prepare for your success. You will find tips and guidance, as well as a step-by-step plan that will help you from start to finish. Here's a more in-depth description of what you will find in this book:

Chapter 1, "Finding Your Way Around: How to Use This Book Effectively": This chapter is an overview of the rest of the book. It gives you a vision of what's in store.

Chapter 2, "Prepare for Success": Chapter 2 is all about preparation. It offers ideas to prepare the environment, both the physical setting of your room and the psychological setting for your participants. It also provides thoughts about how to prepare your participants and clients and, most important, how to prepare yourself for this or any other training event.

Chapter 3, "Tips for Successful Facilitation": Need some tips for better facilitation? This chapter presents tips that you can use during various times of the training cycle. Pick up this chapter and start to read at any point to find a few ideas that you can use.

Chapter 4, "Planning and Preparing for Your Successful Session: How Do I Start?": This is a giant to-do list. It starts from the time you know you will conduct the train-the-trainer and works you all the way through evaluation. This chapter makes the whole process easy to complete.

Chapter 5, "Trainer's Guide: Presenting the Modules and Module 1—Introduction": This chapter introduces module 1 and will help you initiate a successful program. It contains the welcome, objectives, and introduction to the content, as well as detailed step-by-step instructions to help you present the train-the-trainer activities for module 1, identify the equipment and material needs for these activities, and determine the amount of time these activities require.

Chapter 6, "Trainer's Guide: Module 2—Assess and Analyze": This module discusses the importance of assessing learners' needs and ways to gather data. It identifies equipment and material, as well as the amount of time to allot for each activity.

Chapter 7, "Trainer's Guide: Module 3—Design and Develop": This module covers how a training designer, using the data gathered in the needs assessment, creates learning objectives. These objectives provide the foundation for creating a training program to help adult learners gain required skills and knowledge. Instructions are included to help you present the train-the-trainer, identify equipment and materials necessary for the activities, and determine how much time each activity requires.

Chapter 8, "Trainer's Guide: Module 4—Implement and Facilitate": This chapter contains module 4 of the train-the-trainer, which discusses how to facilitate the training session confidently and competently as you keep the focus on the learner. It includes a list of equipment and materials needed, as well as the amount of time to allow.

Chapter 9, "Trainer's Guide: Module 5—Evaluate and Enhance": The final module of the train-the-trainer presents the importance of evaluation, Kirkpatrick's four levels of evaluation, and using what you learn to make improvements. Instructions help you identify equipment and material necessary for the activities, as well as how much time each activity requires.

Chapter 10, "Alternative-Length Delivery Modules": This chapter offers suggestions for shorter modules you might consider for participants who do not need a complete train-the-trainer, but who might need to improve their delivery or to understand their training styles.

Chapter 11, "Participant Materials for a Complete Three-Day Session": Chapter 11 is the complete set of participant materials, or handouts (as thumbnails), which serve as both activity sheets during the session and as resources following the session. Use this chapter as a quick reference to the handouts as you go through the materials. One feature of the materials is the "In Focus," which contains about a half-dozen quick reminders, such as the Good Design ABCs or the 3Cs of a Great Trainer.

Further Reading and Resources: This list includes many books that cover all topics presented in this train-the-trainer, as well as a collection of activity and game books, e-learning books, books about creativity, and books about graphics and design for the trainer. In addition, you'll find resources to help you purchase products such as assessment instruments; clip art; music; paper supplies; props, toys, and training tools; and movies. This section also includes information on licensing and copyright.

The Icons

Icons act as a quick reference. If you use the Trainer's Guide (chapters 5–9) for training, the icons will remind you what you need to do during each activity. Here's the list of icons used in this book:

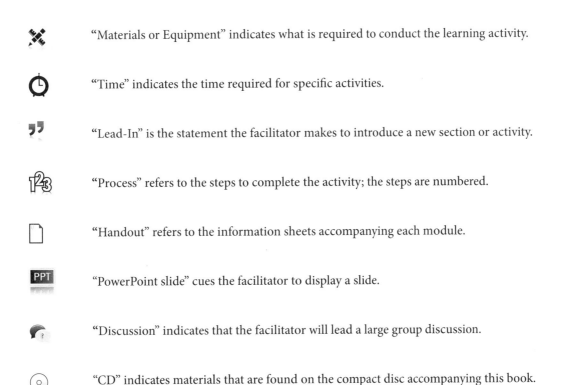

"Materials or Equipment" indicates what is required to conduct the learning activity.

"Time" indicates the time required for specific activities.

"Lead-In" is the statement the facilitator makes to introduce a new section or activity.

"Process" refers to the steps to complete the activity; the steps are numbered.

"Handout" refers to the information sheets accompanying each module.

"PowerPoint slide" cues the facilitator to display a slide.

"Discussion" indicates that the facilitator will lead a large group discussion.

"CD" indicates materials that are found on the compact disc accompanying this book.

What's on the CD?

The materials on the CD are there for your convenience. The CD provides electronic versions of these items:

- the complete Trainer's Guide (chapters 5–9)

- the complete set of participant handouts for the three-day session (use selected handouts for shorter sessions)

- PowerPoint slides

- Session at a Glance (tables 1–5, one for each module)

- equipment and materials packing list

- flipchart preparation and flipcharts (for modules 3 and 4)

- "Team 2 Notes" memo for activity 2-6

- pairwise card set for activity 3-2

- table tent

- train-the-trainer evaluations (2)

- train-the-trainer certificates (2).

Terminology, Jargon, Lingo

It is difficult to select the correct words when you write for learning and development, or training of WLP professionals, or … see what I mean? Readers come from many backgrounds. Some of you are steeped in International Society for Performance Improvement (ISPI) language. Others use Society for Human Resource Management (SHRM) terms. Performance supporters use still another vocabulary. Some people think they have the market on the exact words used. In actuality, the terminology doesn't really matter that much, as long as we can communicate and understand the concepts so we are successful at our jobs.

To set the record straight for those of you who have been around the profession for a while and to clarify the lingo for those of you who are new to the field, here's a list that may help:

Session. I have most often used the word *session,* and I have sprinkled in *workshop* or *program* a few times. You may also find a time or two where I say *the training.* In this situation, I refer specifically to the train-the-trainer training session that you will conduct, whether it is three days or three hours in length. I have also used words such as *learning event, performance improvement,* and even *learning.* I try to avoid *class, course,* or *education* because they sound pedagogical.

Participant. The individual who attends your *session* (see above). I use *participant* most often, but sometimes *learner* seems to be better in the context of the sentence. In other writing, you may see *attendee*, *stakeholder*, *trainee*, and even *student*. I highly recommend that you stay away from *student* because it promotes the concept that the trainer is the knowledgeable one; in fact, we know that is not the case. Our participants have a lot to teach us.

Client. The individual who funds, initiates, or otherwise requests or supports the training session. The individual may be the supervisor of all or some of the participants. For consultants, the client may be the person who hired you to conduct the training session.

Trainer. I tend to use *trainer* and *facilitator* interchangeably. I believe that a trainer must be both. The best trainer is one who uses facilitative skills; however, I do not believe that a facilitator must necessarily use trainer skills. It's a fine point, but I am happy to discuss it with anyone. I feel the same about the word *presenter*. At times, trainers need to be presenters, but presenters do not need to be trainers to be successful at what they do. I avoid using *instructor*, *teacher*, or any other term that leads back to the didactic model of learning. Other terms for trainers include *employee development specialist*, *performance analyst*, *competency expert*, *corporate trainer*, and *performance specialist*.

Methodology. This refers to the type of activities within the training modules that provide the participants with learning experiences. They include things such as role plays, case studies, games, reading, and relay races.

Training room. I actually prefer to just call it *your room*, but that may confuse those new to the profession or those who describe the location of the learning event as a *classroom*. In this book, I use *training room* most often, but sometimes it is awkward and I will revert to *classroom* (even though I don't usually use it when I speak). Some people use *facility* or *venue*.

Handouts. These are the participant materials that serve both as instructions for activities and as resources after the training is over. As a whole, these comprise the participant's manual. Because this book also offers shorter events in module format, all handouts are named and numbered for clear identification.

I am aware that some readers of this book may be new to the profession; therefore, most terms are either defined or self-explanatory. I spell out new acronyms in each chapter, in case someone begins to read the book in the middle. For example, you will see *subject matter expert (SME)* the first time it is mentioned in a chapter, and later I will just use *SME*.

Conclusion

Conducting a train-the-trainer is an honor. It means that you have reached a high level of competence in your career. Others are looking to you for guidance. Congratulations! This book will help you deliver a successful train-the-trainer.

What to Do Next

- If you are an experienced trainer and just need to find good train-the-trainer materials, turn directly to chapter 11, which contains the participant materials to chapters 5 through 9, which constitute the Trainer's Guide. You will find that the numbers and titles of the participant handouts align with the numbers and titles of the activities in the Trainer's Guide.

- If you are an experienced trainer looking for shorter modules for specific competencies, turn to chapter 10, which offers suggested modules for a variety of needs. You may also want to use the participant materials in chapter 11 to create your own modules.

- If you are relatively new to the profession and want some ways to improve your own skills, start with chapters 2 and 3. They discuss the importance of preparation and relate tips and tricks that will help you do a better job of training.

- If you are ready to get started but you are overwhelmed by the hundreds of pages in this book and on the CD, go directly to chapter 4. The step-by-step process will put you at ease. All you need to do is to begin to move down the checklist.

- If you are looking for more resources, turn to Further Reading and Resources, at the end of this book. It is comprehensive and up to date. For a book that aligns directly with the *Ultimate Train-the-Trainer*, pick up a copy of *10 Steps to Successful Training* from ASTD Press.

Prepare for Success 2

What's in This Chapter?

- Ways to set up the training room

- Instructions for preparing equipment and visual aids

- Ways to prepare the participants for a training session

- Instructions for preparing the client

- Ways to prepare for a training session

- Creative ways to practice for the session

▲ ▲ ▲

The Importance of Preparation

If I could change the ADDIE model (see chapter 1 for a discussion of ADDIE; the acronym stands for *a*nalysis, *d*esign, *d*evelopment, *i*mplementation, and *e*valuation), I'd call it ADDPIE—*P* for *p*reparation.

Few trainers put enough emphasis on the preparation required for successful training. I come from the old school, where we learned a 10:1 practice rule: that is, every hour in the classroom required 10 hours of practice. I refer to practicing the presentation only. Those 10 hours do not include room preparation, client preparation, participant preparation, or audiovisual preparation. Yes, that's pretty old school. Today you can hardly find a 1:1 ratio—and it shows!

Well-known trainer Bob Pike believes that 80 percent of what's necessary to be a good trainer and get participant involvement is adequate preparation. In fact, he coined his 6 Ps to remind us of the importance of preparation: "Proper preparation and practice prevent poor performance."

The best thing you can do for your participants is to prepare for their success. If you don't need to worry about your part, you can focus on your participants, which is your most important job.

Training is like an iceberg. Most participants see only the top 10 percent: the error-free PowerPoint slides, the well designed participant materials, a welcoming room setup, your professional facilitation skills, and your organized presentation. It all looks so easy! Consider that a compliment to your preparation.

This chapter will address the other 90 percent, which is below the surface:

- How do you prepare the room and the environment?

- How do you prepare your participants?

- How do you prepare your clients?

- And most important, how do you prepare yourself?

The title of this book is *Ultimate Train-the-Trainer: A Complete Guide to Training Success.* You need to be prepared to succeed. This chapter focuses on preparation.

Prepare the Training Room

When your participants walk into your training room, what do they see? Extra chairs stacked up against a wall? Empty boxes in a corner? Blinds askew? Information technology staff scurrying around, trying to get the projector to work with your computer so you can display your PowerPoint slides? You, thrashing around in your briefcase, looking for your remote? Materials stacked willy-nilly on the tables? Put yourself in your participants' shoes: How would that make you feel? Yes, there will always be times when everything goes wrong, but proper preparation helps you to eliminate most problems.

There are two reasons to spend time preparing the training room:

- Participants will learn better and faster if the training room is conducive to learning. The room should be more than just orderly. We'll address that.

- You will feel more confident in your ability if you are organized. When you don't have to worry about the details of the room, you are better able to meet your participants' needs.

Let's begin with room setup. What's the foundation to any training design? The learning objectives. What's the foundation to how you set up your room? The learning objectives. You can gain this information from the learning objectives:

- how much participation is required

- whether participants will have the best experience working in one team, working with many different people, or a mixture of both

- whether a secondary goal of the session is to get the entire group to work more as a team (that is, a department or functional group)

- whether individual reflection is necessary.

You may not be able to choose your room, so you will have to make do with what you have. When you do have a choice, here are some attributes to consider:

1. *Size and obstructions.* The room should be the appropriate size for the number of participants. If it is too small, everyone will be crammed in, conducting activities will be difficult, and the room will get really hot! If it is too large, building a comfortable, welcoming environment will be difficult—and do you hear that echo, echo, echo? Watch out for pillars in the middle, of course. Windows placed on a west wall without shades will wash out your projected images when the afternoon sun comes streaming in. If the learning objectives require small group work, is there enough room to form small groups that do not disturb others as they are working? If not, request a breakout room or two.

2. *Location.* The room should be in a place that's easy to find, as well as easy to reach, both within the building and also by vehicle. It's not a good start to a day of training to have to park two blocks away and walk in the rain. Ensure that the room is easily accessible to everyone, including those with limited mobility. Check out other features that will enhance your participants' satisfaction, such as the location of water fountains, restrooms, snacks, lunch, and overnight accommodations for those who are from out of town. The convenience will help ensure that participants are satisfied and will return to the room on time after breaks and lunch.

3. *Structure and furniture.* Sometimes the temporary walls in conference centers or hotels are paper thin. If a sales conference is booked next to you, your participants may have difficulty hearing. Check out the furniture that's available. You may have to settle for rectangular tables when you really want round tables. If you are in a hotel, the tables will probably have cloths. Does the hotel staff "skirt" the tables with extra fabric (placed around the edge of the table and extending to the floor)? It covers up marred table legs, but if the fabric gets tangled up in your participants' legs, it becomes a distraction. If your tables do not have tablecloths, make sure they are clean. I've scrubbed some pretty nasty-looking tables in my career. How about the chairs? You'll want to provide the most comfortable chair possible. The ideal training chair should have these features:

   - adjustable height

   - comfortable back

   - upholstered in fabric, not vinyl

   - adjustable arms to relieve body fatigue (ideally, the forearm should be positioned at a 90-degree angle from the upper arm)

   - wheels for moving around

   - ability to swivel, so participants can easily follow the group's conversation

   - seat that is at least 20 inches long and 20 inches wide.

The typical classroom stacking chair meets few of these standards. The room arrangement should satisfy the needs of your agenda. See the seating arrangements in figure 2-1 for several options.

Figure 2-1. Six Common Seating Arrangements

Listed below are six of the most common seating styles for classroom training. They are listed in order of my favorite choices, from first to last. Often you will not have a choice and you will need to make do with what you have.

ARRANGEMENT	GROUP SIZE	ADVANTAGES	DISADVANTAGES
U-Shaped	12–22	Encourages large group discussion, builds the larger team, enables close contact with participants	If a small room, may be difficult to work with those on the other side, linear layout makes eye contact between participants difficult
V-Shaped (V points to front)	Teams of 4–5 and groups of 16–25	Easy to work in table teams, no one has his or her back to back of room, best alternative if using rectangular tables	Some difficulty to promote teamwork among the entire group
Clusters	16–50	Promotes teamwork in each cluster, everyone faces the front if chairs on one side only	Difficult to get participation from those who face the back, some participants may need to move chairs to face the front
Single Round/Square	8–12	Facilitates problem solving, smaller size promotes total involvement, easy for trainer to step out of the action	Media and visual use is difficult, limited group size
Conference	8–12	Moderate communication within group	Maintains trainer as lead, sense of formality, inability for trainer to get close to participants
Classroom	Any size	Traditional, may be expected by learners; trainer controls; participants can view visuals	Low involvement, one-way communication, difficult to form small groups

4. *Electronics.* Ensure that lighting is adequate. Is the light bright enough so that your participants do not fall asleep in a dimly lit, romantic atmosphere? If you're using a PowerPoint presentation, keep in mind that too often trainers dim the lights when it's not necessary. The lumens of light in the projectors used today do not require a darkened room, unlike back in the days of 16mm film. Keep your participants energized and enthused (and awake). The lights should be bright. Having said that, be sure that you know where the light switches are located. Check out the location of outlets and placement of the screen. Will you need to jump over wires throughout the presentation? Even worse, if your participants are expected to present to the group—as they are in a train-the-trainer—loose, untaped cords become a hazard to them.

5. *Climate control.* Much like Goldilocks and the three bears, one-third of your participants will always be too hot, one-third will be too cold, and one-third will be just right. You won't be able to please everyone, but if you have the ability to adjust the temperature yourself, you can try. The day before your session when you are setting up the room, experiment with the controls. Do they respond quickly? Does one degree make a big difference? Do you need to contact someone to help you? Remember, it is usually best to change thermostats one degree at a time. A room that is too cool can quickly become too hot.

6. *Walls.* Do you have adequate wall space on which to hang flipchart pages? Sometimes walls are filled with windows and pictures, which leaves no space to hang anything. On more than one occasion, I have removed the artwork from the walls. The most you will have to deal with is a nail that sticks through a flipchart page. Even if you have adequate wall space, it may not be usable. If the walls are covered with a felt-like fabric, it may be impossible to hang your flipcharts with masking tape. If the flipcharts don't fall down immediately, they will slowly drift down when you are trying to make a critical point. Sometimes you can use thumbtacks on these walls; check it out. At other times, the conference center owners will not allow you to use tape on the walls. For times like these, I carry blue painter's tape. It isn't pretty, but it is guaranteed to leave the paint intact. Finally, make sure that you are using markers that will absolutely not bleed through. The only brand that I know I can count on is Mr. Sketch. Not only that, but they are scented as well—licorice, cinnamon, mint, and, my favorite, cherry!

Prepare Equipment and Visuals

If anything is going to go wrong, it will probably be something related to your equipment or visuals: The projector isn't compatible with your computer, the flipchart doesn't have paper, the DVD player is missing its electrical cord, the extension cord doesn't reach, or your memory stick was damaged in travel. Whatever the problem, it can prevent you from conducting the session that you had envisioned.

Although nothing can ensure that things won't go wrong, following these suggestions will certainly increase your success rate:

1. *Conduct a dry run one week before.* Set up the equipment, go through every PowerPoint slide, prepare your flipchart pages, and check out the visibility. If you have anything tricky, like an embedded video clip, sound bites, or animation, run through it a couple of times. If you have

never used a flipchart, practice flipping, ripping, and hanging techniques. (Have you ever spent a day staring at a flipchart page that isn't straight?) If you have a new remote, try it out, or especially a laser pointer. This is a good time to learn just how far you can stray from your computer while you are using it.

2. *Set up the day before.* Probably your best hedge against something going wrong is to set up the day before. If something is missing, not compatible, or was damaged in transit, you still have time to adjust. Focus all equipment and set the volume appropriately. Check the volume throughout the room, especially if you are relying on a computer for sound, because computers do not have the best sound systems. Turn on everything to ensure that it all works at the same time. Ensure that the projector has the correct lens and that the lens is clean. Check that the screen is large enough and mark the location of the projector with masking tape so that it's easy to reset if it's moved (either because it needs to be locked up or because someone cleaned the floors). Sit in all the seats to be certain that everyone can see the screen, ensuring that, for example, your flipchart stand isn't between one of the participants and the screen. If you are using a computer, be sure that you have the log-in ID and password to access it.

3. *Be prepared for an emergency.* Bring extra batteries for your remote, an extra bulb for the projector, and an extra extension cord for anything electrical. Learn a few troubleshooting tricks for the equipment that you use most often. The next time a technician fixes something, ask what he or she did and why. Pack a roll of duct tape to fasten unruly electrical cords. Be sure that you have the name and contact number (cell phone is best) of the person who will assist you if you are not using your own equipment. Finally, have an alternative plan in case all else fails. All trainers can conduct a successful session without their PowerPoint presentations. You just need to be prepared and think through what you might do ahead of time.

So that takes care of the tangible things you can do to prepare the environment. How about the more personal aspects?

Prepare a Positive Learning Environment

You're going to teach this stuff, so you'd better be modeling it. Focus on your participants' success and create a learning environment of trust and respect. Most of these ideas can be found in another format in chapter 8, **handout 4-3.** They are worth repeating here.

Although these behaviors take place during your session, preparation is critical from two perspectives:

1. It will help you remember to do some of these things.

2. When you're prepared, you won't have to think about setting up the next activity or where you left the special handouts, allowing participants to begin to feel safe, comfortable, and trusting.

The more you demonstrate the listed behaviors, the more people will want to talk with you during the breaks. And the more they talk with you during breaks, the less time you have to prepare for the activities after the break. Therefore, you need to be prepared.

Make the Environment Safe

Every participant will arrive with a different mindset. Your job is to make it safe for everyone to participate. Here are some ideas for how to achieve this:

- Be prepared early enough to greet participants at the door.

- Display a sign or a PowerPoint slide that tells participants they are in the right location and that it's safe to enter the room.

- Learn participants' names and ask them to tell you something about themselves.

- Share the objectives of the training early, so they know what to expect.

- Let participants know WII-FM (what's in it for me).

- Use names and sincere reinforcement to build rapport.

- Learn techniques to get learners to open up.

- Allow participants to evaluate their own learning.

- Create experiential learning activities in which the learners discover their own *aha* moments!

Make the Environment Comfortable

Arrive in a training room early enough to welcome the learners as your guests. Here are some suggestions:

- Ensure that the room is warm, bright, and cheery.

- Have a cup of coffee waiting for them.

- Learn how to adjust the thermostat so that it's comfortable for most participants.

- Ensure that the environment feels comfortable; hide empty boxes, straighten chairs, and place materials neatly at each seat.

- Ensure that all learners can see and hear you and your visuals.

- Plan for ample breaks.

- Share candy, bubble gum, or popcorn.

- Plan celebrations.

Make the Environment Reliable and Trustworthy

Building trust with your participants will make the difference between just attending training and absorbing knowledge. Here are some ways to start:

- Use small breakout groups to overcome participants' early reluctance to share ideas or concerns.

- Use body language to encourage participation; positive nods, smiles, and eye contact all show that you are interested in their ideas.

- Share something about yourself to begin a trusted exchange of ideas.

- Create discussion among the learners.

- Show that you value their opinions and ideas.

- Pair individuals as sounding boards for one another.

Prepare Your Participants

Touch base with your participants before the session. This makes it easier to develop rapport, build trust, clarify the purpose of the training, and initiate the learning. Other than providing a reading assignment that one-third will skim, one-third will forget to do, and one-third will claim they never received, what can you do? These ideas will prepare the participant for the topic and will help them to accept you as a credible resource:

- Email the objectives of the session. Provide a phone number or email address and encourage them to contact you with any questions. Better yet, send a letter or a welcome card that includes the same information.

- Ask participants to complete an action, such as interview a couple of leaders, survey colleagues, or ask co-workers for feedback. For a train-the-trainer session, you could provide three questions to ask current trainers in their work area, ask the participants to bring a design project they are currently completing, or send the participants the self-assessment ahead of time and ask them to complete it before they attend the session.

- Send a cartoon (*Dilbert* has been great), puzzle, brain teaser, or thought-provoking question that is pertinent to the session and that arouses their curiosity.

- Meet their safety needs by sending the logistics of the session: location of the site, room number, telephone number for emergencies, plans for lunch, email access, available parking, available public transportation, a roster of other participants, and other pertinent material that will help them feel comfortable and ready to attend the session.

- Speak with the participants' managers or supervisors to determine what they want the participants to be able to do when they return. Encourage the managers and supervisors to speak with their employees before the session. You may want to include discussion notes for the supervisor to address with the participant.

- Invite participants to send you any pertinent questions or topics they would like you to cover during the session.

- Send the participants a brief questionnaire that focuses on their unique needs; this will get them involved in the agenda early and allow you to customize it for them.

- Conduct a mini needs assessment at www.surveymonkey.com or http://zoomerang.com. Share the results with the participants before the session or early in the session.

- Call participants, introduce yourself, and tell them the objectives and purpose of the course. Ask if they have anything specific that they might like to cover in the session.

- Even though the results of assigned reading are dismal, that should not deter you from considering it.

Prepare Your Client

Perhaps you think preparing your client is unusual. What is the purpose? Remember that your focus is on the participants. Your participants will benefit the most (as will your client) if clear communication exists among you, the participant, and the client. These ideas set the stage to ensure that a transfer of learning will occur:

- Contact your client before you finalize the training plans and ask about issues or concerns that your client hopes to resolve with the training. You may be able to use these ideas to personalize the training or to address special issues. Often the information is just what you need to develop a new role play or critical incident.

- Meet with your client to review the materials. Sometimes the participants' bosses may not agree with a new concept or may not understand it. It's better to discuss this before the training.

- Discuss how your client will support and reinforce the training.

- Offer to coach your client after the training has been completed.

- Before the training occurs, provide a template of a pretraining contract. The client and the participant can spell out exactly what the participant is to learn during the session and implement when he or she returns to work.

- Invite your client to share ideas for his or her vision of the session and then to kick off the session.

Prepare Yourself

The more you have prepared, the more smoothly your session will run and the fewer problems you should encounter. Even if something does go wrong, your preparation will pay off because you will be better able to address the problem.

Prepare for This Train-the-Trainer

My preparation begins the same day I know I will conduct the training. At that time, I put it on my calendar, open a file, and pull the materials (if I have presented the session in the past) or begin to stack books or articles I might use as resources if it is a new session.

For those of you who know you are going to conduct the train-the-trainer you now hold in your hands, continue to read. Once you've completed this chapter, peruse chapter 1 so you are familiar with how the book is organized. Next, read all the participant handouts (see chapter 11 and the accompanying CD). The content is important to you in two ways:

1. It is the content you will teach.

2. It is the content you must model as you teach—a training within the training.

Let that content gurgle around a bit. Take a break from train-the-trainer and, in a week or so, scan the participant handouts again and then put them beside the Trainer's Guide as you read it. The PowerPoint slides don't contain a lot of information, so they will not be very valuable if you are learning content. They will help you organize, however. Organize your thoughts now and organize your presentation later. Next, complete the following exercise.

Materials to Collect for This Exercise

• module 3, **handouts 3-13** through **3-17**

• module 2, **handout 2-6**

Step-by-Step Instructions

1. Complete the questionnaire that identifies your training style (module 3, **handouts 3-13** through **3-17**). Take 90 minutes to read, absorb, complete the activity, and conduct some self-reflection.

2. Next, I suggest that you complete the Participant's Personal Needs Assessment (module 2, **handout 2-6**). This will give you a good idea not only of your skill level, but also of the modules that may be the most difficult for you to deliver. If you decide to strengthen your skills a bit, I suggest that you read a copy of *Training for Dummies* (Biech, 2005) or *10 Steps to Successful Training* (Biech, 2009).

    You've been buried in the details. Now it's time to lift yourself above it all and look at the train-the-trainer from the big-picture perspective. Look at the "Session at a Glance" in chapters 5–9 and on the CD. Print a copy for yourself and fill in the actual times your session will run. Run your final copy of this schedule on brightly colored paper (I like a bright yellow) so that you can always find it on your training table. This task will give you a better idea of the general topics you will complete in large chunks.

If you are not going to do the complete three-day session, it's time for you to determine which alternative agendas you might conduct. You will find them in chapter 10.

Once you know what you will present, make a copy of the handouts you will use. Add your notes and begin to practice with the PowerPoint slides. If you need some ideas for how you might practice, I have provided a list near the end of this chapter.

A complete to-do list for this train-the-trainer can be found in chapter 4.

General Preparation for You

Here's a quick checklist of what I do to prepare before every training session:

• Review the training session thoroughly and list all the logistical details that need to be addressed. Create a checklist of these details and begin to address the items at least one week before the session.

- About this same time, create a packing list of all the things you need to take to the training session with you.

- Complete all participant materials and visuals early enough so that someone else can proofread them, and you have time to make corrections. For this train-the-trainer, you will need to print out the participant handouts from the CD. I suggest that you use a three-hole punch and put them in a binder. You will also use evaluations, certificates, flipcharts, the "Team 2 Notes" memo for activity 2-6, the pairwise card set for activity 3-2, and table tents. You will need to locate resources (either articles or *Infolines*) for the Skill Practice in activity 4-9 (chapter 8).

- Learn who is in your session to help you customize and plan the focus of your training. You might be able to learn each person's position, understanding of the subject, reasons for attending, opinions, and concerns.

- Check on your room about one week before your session. This will alert you to any problems with rescheduling or double booking with other groups.

- Provide a detailed drawing of how you want the room to be set up. Don't assume, however, that it will be correct. I change my room set up more often than not. It seems that if you ask for a room to be set up for 20, the facilities staff thinks that more is better and will set it up for 25. Then it appears as though you had a lot of "no-shows."

- Begin to make contact with those in charge of the logistics at least one week in advance of your session to confirm that they have your requests on record. Contact them again the day before, reminding them that you intend to arrive either two hours before the session begins or the night before to finalize the logistics. Remind them that you will want your audiovisuals set up so you can try them out. Make sure you have the name and phone number of the contact person who will let you into the room.

- Set up the room the day (or evening) before the session. Part of my preparation is setting up the room. People often offer to help, but I prefer to do it myself; the process helps me feel prepared. I know where things are, and I know whether I have forgotten something. It's a great way for me to give the room my personal touch, take ownership of the space, and prepare to welcome my guests the next day.

- Arrive one to two hours before the session begins to set up materials, finish last-minute details, tidy the room, rearrange furniture, set up and test equipment, and handle anything else that crops up.

- Due to the possibility of eleventh-hour crises, be sure that you are fully prepared and rehearsed and that your materials are in ready-to-go order.

No amount of preparation will avert all problems, but the more you prepare, the better you will be able to address any problems that do arise. You can find a more detailed checklist called, "The Procrastinator's Lifeline," in figure 2-2 on the following page.

Figure 2-2. The Procrastinator's Lifeline

Are you a procrastinator like me? Don't have time to read this entire step? Here's a quick-and-dirty checklist of what you need to do and when you need to do it.

One Week Before
- Practice your session in front of a colleague; ask for input, feedback, and ideas.
- Know your subject cold. Your confidence will grow if you do.
- Memorize the words you intend to use during the first five minutes. The first few minutes are usually the most nerve wracking for a trainer.
- Make a list of things you want to remember to do or pack for the session: equipment, supplies, notes on how to set up the room and what you will place at each participant's seat, names and phone numbers of people who will support the session in any way (for example, the person who has the key to the training room), and so forth.
- If you asked participants to complete a survey or other prework, check that you have all the responses.
- Confirm all room arrangements, refreshments, equipment, and supplies.

One Day Before
- Run through the entire session, practicing with visuals.
- Confirm that you have enough participant materials and all of your supplies.
- Check that you have your Trainer's Guide or notes and keep it with you to take to the session.
- Check on everything you need regarding the training site, including location of restrooms, refreshments, support staff, and so forth.
- Set up the training room, placing tables and chairs strategically to encourage participation.
- Observe the room's mechanics. Will lighting cause any problems? Windows facing east or west? Look for the light switches. Figure out where the thermostat is located and whether you have any control over it.

- Set up your equipment, marking placement of the projection table with masking tape on the floor. Test the equipment. Run through Power-Point slides one last time to ensure they are in order. Practice with the actual equipment. Do you know how to use the wireless remote control? Where is the reverse button? Can you roll the pages on the flipchart smoothly?
- Arrange the participants' materials on their tables. Place the training manuals, pens, agendas, table tents, markers, and anything else each participant needs neatly at each seat. Place other shared materials for small group activities or exercises in the center of round tables, or equally spaced around a U or other linear placement. These items may include sticky notes, index cards, handouts, or paper.
- Take one last look around. Empty boxes in the front of the room? Get rid of them. Don't depend on the clean-up crew to discard them for you.
- Get a good night's sleep.

One to Two Hours Before
- Arrive at the training site at least one hour before start time.
- Complete last-minute set up.
- Organize the space from which you will train:
  ◦ Are your notes in order, turned to the first page, placed where you can stay organized?
  ◦ Is your visual support in order, placed where you want it?
  ◦ Do you have a glass of water?
  ◦ Do you have a few paper towels for an emergency?
  ◦ Are tools and supplies where you want them: markers on the flipchart tray, pencil near your notes, sticky notes and index cards at the side, and completed table tent at the front of the table?
  ◦ Have you ensured cords are covered or taped down?

continued on next page

Figure 2-2. The Procrastinator's Lifeline, *continued*

- Ensure media equipment placement is correct, tested, and set to first slide.
- Make yourself comfortable: Use the restroom, get a drink of water.
- Move around the room and greet people as they arrive until two to five minutes before start time.

One Minute Before
- Take one more peek at your opening line.
- Take a deep breath.

- Tell yourself how phenomenal this is going to be.
- Find a friendly face.
- Smile.
- Go for it!

There you have it—the long and the short of preparation, that is.

Identify Ways to Practice for Your Train-the-Trainer

Practice makes perfect—or so my grandmother would say. As a trainer, you have lots of things to practice. You can start with these:

- Practice setting up and debriefing the activities with colleagues.

- Practice the mechanics, especially if you need to use two kinds of audiovisuals at the same time.

- Practice the theatrics if you plan to tell a story with a punch line that needs certain pauses or inflections. Tell your story to colleagues or friends to get feedback.

- Practice aloud to ensure that you have no enunciation problems.

- Practice in the room where you will conduct the training so that you feel comfortable—so comfortable it becomes *your* room.

- Anticipate the questions participants may ask, as well as your responses to them.

- Practice the questions you will ask participants.

- Practice in several different ways:
  - in front of a mirror
  - for your colleagues
  - for your family, friends—even your dog (who will make great eye contact!)
  - with a tape recorder
  - in front of a camera.

Practice and preparation can make your training session all that you had hoped it would be.

Tips for Successful Facilitation   3

What's in This Chapter?

- Easy ways to improve facilitation techniques
- Tips to improve personal skills

Thousands of tips exist in hundreds of books about how to be an excellent facilitator, yet most of them can be reduced to two basic cautions:

- Be prepared.
- Put your participants first.

You read about being prepared in the last chapter, so in this chapter we'll focus more on putting your participants first. Of course, most of these suggestions will require some preparation on your part.

This chapter could easily be an entire book, so instead of long paragraphs with a beginning, middle, and an end, think of this chapter as a collection of trainer tips. Let's present these tips based on the four phases in the training cycle created for this book:

- Assess and Analyze
- Design and Develop
- Implement and Facilitate
- Evaluate and Engage.

As you read through the list, you may want to place a check next to those skills that you have mastered. Those you have not mastered—or perhaps not even thought about—may require either self-reflection or additional research. The reading list at the end of this book will help you locate other ideas. In addition, I will mention some of the authors who are worth pursuing for additional insight in particular topics.

Your facilitation success starts before you enter the training room. It begins the day that you accept (or are assigned) the task of conducting this train-the-trainer workshop. Let's begin with Assess and Analyze.

Assess and Analyze

The successful facilitator is aware of the needs assessment and the purpose of the training session. Even if you did not conduct the assessment or analysis, obtain a copy of the written report that outlines why the outcome is important to your organization. If the training has been around a long time, learn about the evaluation results, feed that information to the front end of the process, and suggest modifications as appropriate. Get to know your business and your leaders so that you have the kind of fundamental knowledge that builds your analytical skills. Here are some practices that you may wish to use in the future:

- No matter how extensive and complete your assessment and analysis are, it is always a good idea to conduct a mini needs assessment with participants at the beginning of each session. "What are your hopes and fears for this session?" "How much experience do you have with …?" This does two things. First, it helps determine whether the design is on the mark. Second, it gives participants an opportunity to state their expectations and to begin to participate early.

- If time is limited and you are unable to conduct a full-blown needs analysis, you may still want to gather some data. To do this, speak to your contact person, talk to several participants, email a simple questionnaire, ask your contact person to provide materials that are relevant to the session, or contact other trainers who have worked with the group.

- Check with your local college or university. Marketing classes are often looking for assessment or survey design projects. You may need to allow time for the design, as well as time to educate the group or individual about your organization. If you have time but a minimum amount of money, this can be an elegant solution.

Design and Develop

If you are not a designer of training, this step has often been completed by the time you are assigned to deliver the training session. The book you are holding, for example, appears to be complete; however, training design and material development are rarely perfect for every group. The suggestions gathered in the Assess and Analyze section give you some ways you might tweak the materials or the activities. However, if you are a designer, remember that the design should be built on a foundation formed by two important aspects: adult learning principles and the learning objectives. Whether you are the designer/developer or the facilitator/trainer, you are responsible for being sure that the program meets the needs of the participants, is both fun and functional, and solves a concern or problem in your organization. Here are some points to remember:

- If objectives are not specific enough, there will be a lot of room for individual interpretation.

- When you write objectives, remember to

- Be brief and to the point; include only one major item in each objective.

- Use an observable action verb to describe the expected result. You can see or hear when someone lists, demonstrates, or calculates. You cannot see someone remember, believe, or learn.

- Ensure that your objectives are realistic and can reasonably be accomplished in the time allotted; you must also have the necessary resources to accomplish these objectives.

- Post the objectives at the beginning of your sessions.

- The design should include a variety of training methodologies to keep participants interested.

- To help participants meet everyone in the group, include a variety of groupings: pairs, trios, pair with someone at another table, table teams, two teams, and individual reflection.

- Use an icebreaker with a return-on-investment (ROI); for example, use an icebreaker for participants to get to know each other that also allows you to learn about their expectations and gets them started on the topic.

- Include transitions in your design; the biggest problems happen in sports during the handoffs. Don't let the same thing occur when you hand off one topic to the next.

- Make the design interesting, memorable, and practical; your participants will thank you for it.

- Create pre-session assignments in which participants gather data that can be used during session activities.

- Games should have simple instructions, add energy as well as enable learning, and be right for the audience. Be sure to allow enough time for both the game and the debriefing.

- Determine how you will promote networking among participants.

- Build a prop into your session to help people remember key points.

Implement and Facilitate

The implementation is the aspect of training that most people, especially your participants, think of when they hear the word *training*. It's the part that they experience and the part that they'll judge as useful or worthless, practical or unrealistic, a horrible experience or a quality experience. Use these tricks during the train-the-trainer workshop to obtain more votes on the positive side of the ledger:

- Build credibility with your participants subtly. No one likes a braggart, but you can often mention a book you've written or an award you've been given in your introduction, or include it in an example that you use or in an activity.

- Set ground rules up front.

- Identify their expectations and share your expectations early.

- Remember participant names; it's easy if you have a sketch of the room setup. As individuals introduce themselves, add their names to your sketch.

- Begin to use participants' names as soon as they introduce themselves. It helps participants feel welcome and helps you remember their names.

- Use *we* rather than *I* when discussing the session, for example, "Let's go over the objectives," instead of "I'll review the objectives for you."

- Tell participants that this is their learning room and that you want it to be comfortable for them (temperature, lighting, noise, distractions, and so forth).

- Set a goal that everyone will speak at least twice in the first hour.

- When you discuss administrative needs, avoid calling it *housekeeping*; the term is old, overused, and passé.

- Act upbeat, even if you are not up to par every day.

- Never underestimate the power of enthusiasm; it's infectious. Humor covers a great deal.

- Facilitation requires good communication skills: attending, observing, listening, and questioning.

- Be aware of your nonverbal behavior.

- No one wants to listen to a person with *I* trouble.

- Generally, your preferred training and facilitation style will be congruent with your preferred learning style. This means that your training style may clash with some of the participants' learning styles. For example, if a participant favors an independent, kinesthetic style and you have lectured for the past hour, chances are you have lost the participant.

- When participants share stories or problems, remember to use them as examples later on in the session.

- Add fun to function during large group discussions:

  ◦ Encourage repeated audience responses, such as cheers.

  ◦ Get participants involved to demonstrate your point.

  ◦ Ask for a show of hands in response to questions.

  ◦ Ask for people to stand or sit in response to questions.

  ◦ Use a humorous anecdote or read a cartoon that makes your point.

  ◦ Tell a story, recite a poem, or quote someone important.

- Even if your session is well planned, you may find it necessary to make adjustments on the spot. Perhaps participants know more or less than you expected, or the method you are using is not working. If you find yourself in this situation, ask yourself these three questions:

- If I stick with the presentation as planned, what is the likely result?

- If I change the plan, what are the likely consequences?

- Given the purpose and the participants, which is the preferred route?

- Invite questions.

- Subgroups need your attention. Walk around, ensure that they understand the directions and are not getting sidetracked, and determine how much more time they need.

- Don't hesitate to say, "I don't know." Continue with, "Does anyone else know?" And then, "I will find out and get back to you by _____."

- Conduct a round robin early to get participation from everyone.

- When you ask a question, wait for an answer.

- Create opportunities for participants to discover knowledge by themselves.

- Accept that participants may not always agree with you.

- Accept ideas and accept feelings.

- Debrief all activities; consider at the minimum using the "what?," "so what?," and "now what?" model.

Evaluate and Enhance

The last step in the process is to evaluate the results and enhance the effort for the next time. This is the area in which many of us in the field fall short. It certainly isn't due to a shortage of information or models. Books are published; Jack Phillips alone pops one or two out every year. Conferences are held; international conferences feature evaluation topics, and niche conferences spring up around the world. Articles are written (and we assume read), classes are taken, and electronic resources are searched. Then what's the problem? It seems that evaluation has not become routine for many organizations, yet it's necessary that evaluation becomes an integral part of the training cycle. The information must be seen as an important part of the process. No matter where your organization stands in the evaluation debate, as a trainer/facilitator you can do your part to disseminate information about the importance of evaluation. In addition, you can model the need for continued evaluation by using some of these ideas:

- Circle back to your objectives when you develop your evaluation.

- Learn the art and science of tying results to the bottom line.

- Share results with your clients and your participants.

- Use a flipchart for a quick evaluation at the end of a short session. Draw a large T-grid with the words *works well* on one side and *need to improve* on the other side. Then ask for ideas from your participants.

- Allow for anonymity to receive honest answers.

- Keep copies of your evaluations. Use the ideas and suggestions they contain to improve your future performance and program designs.

- Pilot all tests before you use them with participants.

- Meet with supervisors after the training to determine how much of the learning was transferred to the workplace.

- Work with key leaders to identify how training affects the bottom line.

- Consider conducting a focus group with key supervisors if a training session will be repeated. They can tell you which skills seem to be transferring to the workplace and which ones are not.

The Last Word: Focus to Enhance Your Skills

Finally, evaluate and invest in you: your skills, your knowledge, and your mindset. Select one of the ideas that you did not check off from this list and determine how you might improve. Consider these other steps you can take to enhance your skills and identify more on your own:

- Identify the skills required to build a partnership with the managers and supervisors.

- Learn more about ROI; for example, take a class with Jack Phillips.

- Consider getting your certification (the Certified Professional in Learning and Performance [CPLP] credential) from ASTD.

- Join a professional organization. ASTD comes to mind first, but another one that is related to your organization's work would also be practical.

- Attend ASTD's annual International Conference & Exposition. Every trainer should do this at least once; you will learn a great deal.

- Network with other trainers inside and outside your organization. You can call on them when you have a question.

- Read. Read to stay on top of what's new. Read to learn new techniques. Read to locate fresh ideas. Read business and training books, technical and professional journals, and blogs and websites on-line. Read. (See the Further Reading and Resources list at the back of the book.)

- Observe someone else conduct training to obtain new techniques.

- Train with a partner and provide feedback to each other.

- Provide demonstrations for specific activities to other trainers to obtain feedback.

- Enroll in another train-the-trainer workshop—preferably one in which you are videotaped—and obtain feedback on your training style.

- Pay attention to what your customers (the participants) tell you on the evaluation. Make appropriate changes.

- Be aware of your customers' changing needs. Adapt the material and the sessions to them.

- Experiment with activities you've never tried before, perhaps something from a book by Thiagi or Mel Silberman.

- Learn how to conduct a true experiential learning activity (ELA); check the *Pfeiffer Annuals*.

Planning and Preparing for Your Successful Session: How Do I Start?

4

What's in This Chapter?

- The process of conducting a training session
- A specific step-by-step process to implement this train-the-trainer
- A dozen ways to practice any material
- Suggestions for selecting a room
- A list of all the materials required to conduct activities included in the Trainer's Guide (chapters 5–9)

Getting Started

Help! I am overwhelmed! How do I get started?

I opened chapter 2 wistfully wishing that I could change the ADDIE model (see chapter 1 for a discussion of ADDIE; the acronym stands for *a*nalysis, *d*esign, *d*evelopment, *i*mplementation, and *e*valuation) to ADDPIE and add a *P* for preparation. This chapter puts into practice what chapter 2 presents as advice. It will follow the ADDPIE model, laying out step by step (and in some instances, day by day) everything you need to do to demonstrate competence and confidence.

If you are not a new trainer, then you are used to planning and preparation when you conduct a training session and you probably do most of what is listed in this chapter. Good for you! Skim this list of actions, and perhaps you will glean a few new tidbits that will save you time or trouble.

If you are an experienced trainer but have always trained from your own material, or if you have never used an all-inclusive training guide like this, it can be daunting to approach one of these tomes! If that is the case, perhaps you found your way to this chapter because of the title. I suggest you read chapter 1 first. It will provide you with the roadmap you need to find your way around this train-the-trainer guide.

An Action List for Your Success

The goal of this comprehensive action list is to help you plan for your first successful training session. More details may be listed than you ever thought you needed! Follow the list and check off the items to ensure that you won't forget anything during your planning and will thus be truly prepared. Items are spread out over a couple of months because I am sure you have other things to do besides prepare for your train-the-trainer session.

You Just Learned That You Will Conduct a Train-the-Trainer Session

☐ Confirm the date, time, and location for the training.

☐ Place the event on your calendar.

☐ Copy this checklist to guide your actions.

☐ Start a file and place the materials in it. See the "Equipment and Materials List" at the end of this chapter.

☐ Find out if you can experience the training session as a participant before you conduct it.

☐ Start to collect books or articles you may wish to use as resources.

☐ Review this entire checklist so you have an idea of what's ahead.

☐ Peruse chapter 1 so you are familiar with how this book is organized.

☐ Print a copy of chapters 5, 6, 7, 8, and 9 for yourself from the CD; label the chapters appropriately and place them in a three-ring binder. Also print a set of the participant handouts and a copy of the Session at a Glance from the CD. This becomes your Trainer's Guide.

☐ Reserve the training room, providing a diagram of the room setup (remember to plan for breakout rooms on the morning of Day 3). See "Room Selection Recommendations" later in this chapter.

☐ Create a participant list with all contact information.

☐ Schedule participants and introduce yourself to them if necessary.

☐ Begin to create your own list of logistical steps to take as required by your organization:

- Arrange for refreshments and meals.

- Plan travel for participants, such as hotel rooms.

- Reserve equipment, such as projector, screen, computer, and flipcharts.

Ten Weeks Before Your Session

☐ Read all the participant handouts that you copied from the CD. The content is important to you in two ways:

1. It is the content you will teach.

2. It is the content you must model as you teach—a training within the training.

☐ Complete all the activities in the participant materials (in a few rare cases you may need to refer to the Trainer's Guide in chapters 5 through 9).

☐ Focus on the activities in **handouts 3-13** through **3-17** to determine your training style.

☐ Complete the Participant's Personal Needs Assessment (**handout 2-6**) to give you an idea of skills you need to develop a bit; consider reading a copy of *Training for Dummies* (Biech, 2005), or *10 Steps to Successful Training* (Biech, 2009).

☐ Review the resources and books you collected.

☐ Schedule a meeting with your client to determine the desired outcomes of the training session.

Eight Weeks Before Your Session

☐ Scan the participant materials.

☐ Read the Trainer's Guide in chapters 5 through 9 and review the PowerPoint slides at the same time.

☐ Identify the support materials on the CD.

Seven Weeks Before Your Session

☐ Place the participant handouts next to the facilitator's guide and begin to envision what you will do and what you will say in the session.

☐ Use your client's input to determine whether you need to customize any of the materials.

☐ Decide whether you need to customize any of the participant materials in chapter 11 and on the CD.

☐ Make required changes to the participant materials.

☐ If you are not going to conduct the complete three-day session, determine which alternative agendas you might use (see chapter 10).

☐ Print an original of the participant materials after you have customized them.

☐ Ask someone to proofread the participant materials.

☐ Select the evaluation that you wish to use from the CD (customize if necessary).

☐ Print copies of the table tents, evaluations, memos, and pairwise cards from the support materials on the CD.

☐ Arrange to have the participant materials copied and placed in three-ring binders; add a cover and dividers, to create Participant Guides.

☐ Transfer the PowerPoint slides to a memory stick or your computer so you can begin to work with them.

☐ Look at the "Session at a Glance," which you printed from the CD.

Six Weeks Before Your Session

☐ Make any travel arrangements.

☐ Customize your notes:

- Decide whether you will train from the Trainer's Guide or the participant materials (do not try to do both).

- Add your personal stories and examples.

- Think about transitions from one topic to the next.

- Use a highlighter for key words.

☐ Review the copy of the "Session at a Glance" from the CD and fill in the actual times, as well as where you intend to take lunch or short breaks. Print your final copy of this schedule on brightly colored paper so you can always find it on your training table.

☐ Begin to use your notes and the PowerPoint slides. Several ideas for how you might practice are listed near the end of this chapter.

☐ Create a packing list; start with the equipment and materials packing list provided at the end of this chapter and on the CD, and add items as necessary.

☐ Review the logistical details that need to be addressed; is everything on target?

☐ Locate resources for the Skill Practice activity (activities 4-9 and 4-10); see chapter 8.

☐ Contact participants and conduct a mini assessment: What do they want to achieve in the session? Learn their position, their understanding of the subject, the reasons they are attending, their opinions, and any problems they may bring with them or concerns you might encounter.

Four Weeks Before Your Session

☐ Check that the room arrangements are still confirmed (rooms are often rescheduled); at this point, you still have time to find alternative accommodations.

☐ Inform audiovisual support staff what time you want audiovisual equipment set up and in place (at least two hours before you start, or the day before, if possible, so you can rehearse).

☐ Conduct a dry run of the activities that you are most unsure of with your colleagues.

Two Weeks Before Your Session

☐ Use the packing list to begin to pack supplies and materials.

☐ Continue to practice the material.

☐ Back up your PowerPoint slides to a memory stick or CD; send the slides to yourself in an email as an extra precaution.

One Week Before

☐ Confirm all participants who will attend, including those who have been added.

☐ Check on the logistics and confirm room setup and refreshments using final participant numbers.

☐ Confirm the time that the audiovisual equipment will be in place.

☐ Obtain the names and phone numbers of the people who will be in charge of setting up the room, providing audiovisual support and refreshments, and opening the room early; try to get cell phone numbers, if possible.

☐ Customize and print certificates with individuals' names; get them signed and dated.

☐ Practice your session in front of a colleague and ask him or her for input, feedback, and ideas.

☐ Memorize the words you intend to use during the first five minutes, which is often the most difficult time for trainers.

☐ Know your subject cold; your confidence will grow if you do.

☐ Make your personal list of things you will want to remember to do or pack for the session: equipment, supplies, how to set up the room, what you will place at each participant's seat, and the names and phone numbers of all people who will support the session (for example, the person who has the key to the training room).

☐ Check to be sure you have all participants' responses if you asked them to complete a survey or other prework.

☐ Decide how you can work in any expectations from participants.

One Day Before

☐ Run through the entire session; practice with PowerPoint slides and the flipchart.

☐ Check the "Session at a Glance," to ensure that you are prepared for everything.

☐ Confirm that you have enough participant materials and all of your supplies.

☐ Check that you have your Trainer's Guide or notes and keep it with you to take to the session.

☐ Check on everything you need regarding the training site, including location of restrooms, emergency exits, refreshments, support staff, and so forth.

☐ Set up the training room, placing tables and chairs to encourage participation; recommended setup for this session is round tables of four to five participants each.

☐ Observe the room's mechanics:

- Will lighting cause any problems?
- Do windows face east or west?

- Where are the light switches located?

- Where is the thermostat, and do you have any control over it?

☐ Set up your equipment and screen, and mark the placement of the projector with masking tape (in case it gets bumped or moved overnight).

☐ Test the equipment. Load and run through the PowerPoint slides one last time to ensure that they are in order. Practice with the actual equipment. Do you know how to use the wireless remote control? Where is the reverse button? Can you roll the pages on the flipchart smoothly?

☐ Prepare preprinted flipchart pages (see Flipchart Preparation on the CD).

☐ Create and hang the parking lot flipchart page.

☐ Position all flipcharts so you can use them, participants can see them, and they do not block vision to the screen; place appropriate colors of markers in tray.

☐ Arrange the participants' materials on their tables:

- Place participant manuals, pens, agendas, table tents, and markers neatly at each seat.

- Place other shared materials in the center of the tables, including sticky notes, index cards, tactile items, crayons, and paper.

☐ Take one last look around and remove empty boxes from the front of the room.

☐ Get a good night's sleep.

One to Two Hours Before

☐ Arrive at the training site at least one hour before start time; two hours is even better.

☐ Complete last-minute setup.

☐ Organize the space from which you will train:

- Notes are in order, turned to the first page, and placed where you can stay organized.

- Visual support is placed where you want it.

- Water is available.

- A few paper towels are available in case of an emergency.

- Tools and supplies are where you want them: markers on the flipchart tray, pencil near your notes, and sticky notes and index cards at the side.

- Your table tent is completed and placed at the front as a model.

- Cords are covered or taped down.

☐ Ensure media equipment placement is correct, tested, and set to the first slide.

☐ Display your welcome slide.

☐ Make yourself comfortable—use the restroom and get a drink of water.

☐ Move around the room to greet people as they arrive, until two to five minutes before the training session begins.

One Minute Before

☐ Take one more peek at your opening line.

☐ Take a deep breath.

☐ Tell yourself how phenomenal this is going to be.

☐ Find a friendly face.

☐ Smile.

☐ Go for it!

Additional Tips and Lists

Use the tips and lists included in this section for additional success.

Personalize the Session

The theme is focus, so anything you can do to illustrate the theme will help to pull the session together. You can purchase inexpensive magnifying glasses from a place like Oriental Trading Company (see the resource list at the end of this book); bring your own focus materials, such as glasses or microscopes; or add sketches of a magnifying glass to flipchart pages. All of these things will help carry out the theme.

A Dozen Ways to Practice Any Material

Most of us don't have enough time to practice. These suggestions might help you find some extra time:

☐ Practice the entire program *at least once* out loud and ideally in the room where you will present.

☐ Set up your camcorder and record the entire program. You are your own best critic; you will find all kinds of things you would like to do better.

☐ Memorize the first couple of paragraphs you will say. Most trainers stop feeling nervous after five to 15 minutes.

☐ Practice in front of a mirror; many trainers swear by this method. Look yourself in the eye and train away.

☐ Make an audio recording of yourself. If you record yourself on a CD, you can listen to it while you are driving or doing other things. You can also critique your speed, clarity, and articulation.

☐ Transfer your recording to your iPod and listen while you are walking on the treadmill or running.

☐ Practice the activities with colleagues and ask for a critique. What went well? What do they think you could do better?

☐ Practice using the visuals. Practice several times with the audiovisual equipment you will use.

☐ Practice with your equipment. Practice using your remote. Practice turning the slides on and off. Practice starting your equipment.

☐ Practice out loud. Practice pronouncing difficult words. Practicing aloud gives you the opportunity to time your presentations.

☐ Present some of the material to your spouse, significant other, or your dog. Really! Dogs make great eye contact, and some will listen forever, giving you only positive nonverbal feedback.

Get practice in front of groups in other ways, as well. You could try out for a play; join Toastmasters, the National Speakers Association, or other speaking groups; accept a club office; or volunteer to give toasts for special occasions.

Room Selection Recommendations

Because of the unique nature of the training, you need to take care with room selection. I recommend that you train no more than 20 people per session.

Set up your room with four round tables. You will also need an additional table in the front of the room on which to place your Trainer's Guide and other materials.

In addition to the right size, select a room with these characteristics:

☐ There are no posts or barriers that may block the view.

☐ It has wall space for posting flipchart paper.

☐ It has sufficient lighting (preferably natural light), ventilation, and temperature controls.

☐ Restrooms, telephones, and refreshments are located nearby.

☐ It has space for four breakout sessions on Day 3.

Set up your room the day or evening before the session; this gives you time to locate anything that may have been forgotten. You will be much more relaxed the next day. It also prevents that last-minute rush to get everything done.

Something that is nice to do, but not necessary, is to display some books or journals about training. This often encourages participants to continue to learn on their own after the session. The resources can also stimulate interesting discussions among the participants, as well as with you.

Equipment and Materials List

Refer to these equipment and materials lists during your preparation, for best results.

Equipment

Here's some equipment you will need for this session:

☐ LCD projector and screen

☐ computer loaded with the PowerPoint slides

☐ remote, to advance slides and extra batteries

☐ projector, which should be placed on a table (as opposed to the projection cart that is usually delivered with it) so that you have room for supplies, Trainer's Guide, a glass of water, and other materials

☐ four to five flipchart stands with full pads of paper; bring one for your preprinted flipcharts and keep the other blank to use spontaneously, as needed; you should have extras for participant presentations on Day 3

☐ an extension cord and an extra projector bulb, just in case

☐ optional: whiteboard, DVD player, or other equipment as appropriate for your participants for activity 4-8 (see chapter 8).

Materials—General

☐ markers for trainer

☐ masking tape

☐ Trainer's Guide (see chapters 5–9)

☐ index cards

☐ PowerPoint presentation.

Materials—For Facilitator

☐ "Team 2 Notes" memo for activity 2-6 (on CD)

☐ pairwise card set for activity 3-2 (on CD)

☐ backup to the PowerPoint slides on your computer, on a CD or a memory stick

☐ articles or *Infoline*s for the Skill Practice in activities 4-9 and 4-10

☐ large bag of M&Ms, popcorn, bubble gum, or other prizes.

Materials—For Each Table

☐ crayons

☐ markers for table tents

☐ colorful sticky notes in various sizes

☐ index cards

☐ Play-Doh, Koosh balls, or other tactile items

☐ inexpensive magnifying glasses to carry out the focus theme.

Materials—For Each Participant

☐ table tent

☐ Participant Guide

☐ envelope to mail congratulatory card

☐ certificate

☐ evaluation.

Trainer's Guide: Presenting the Modules and Module 1—Introduction

5

What's in This Chapter?

- A general introduction to the modules introduced in chapters 5 through 9
- Detailed step-by-step instructions for presenting the train-the-trainer learning activities for Module 1—Introduction
- Instructions for identifying the equipment and material needs for these activities
- Instructions for determining the amount of time these activities require

▲   ▲   ▲

Introducing the Modules

This chapter will help you facilitate a successful program. The content is organized for your convenience. Together with chapters 6 through 9, it contains all the activities required to conduct a three-day train-the-trainer session. The Trainer's Guide is divided into five modules:

1. Introduction (chapter 5)
2. Assess and Analyze (chapter 6)
3. Design and Develop (chapter 7)
4. Implement and Facilitate (chapter 8)
5. Evaluate and Enhance (chapter 9).

Each module includes all the activities needed to complete that particular module.

What's in Each Activity?

Each activity begins with a header that acts as the summary for the activity. The header describes the following:

- *Activity.* This is the name and number of the activity. It matches the name of the handout(s) that your participants will use during the training session.

- *Handouts.* Here you'll find the number(s) of the handout(s) required to conduct the activity. In most cases, only one handout is listed; however, on occasion, when two or more handouts are closely related, they may all be found in one activity. The handout numbering system is easy to understand. The first number (1 through 5) refers to the module, and the second number refers to the placement of the handout in the module. So, handout 3-13 is the 13th handout in Module 3—Design and Develop. Handouts can be found in chapter 11 and on the CD.

- *Materials/Equipment.* Here you will find the required materials—such as index cards, markers, or tape—you might need. If the list requires anything special, such as certificates, evaluations, instructions for participants, cards, or table tents, you can locate a master in the support material on the CD. The equipment is most often a flipchart. A projector to show the slides is not listed because it is needed throughout the entire session.

- *Slides.* The slides are numbered in order by module (like the handouts) and listed in this header; you can download them from the CD. You can also customize them as you wish.

- *Time.* This is how many minutes the activity should take. If the activity is long or has several segments within it, you will also find a reference to time in the process steps.

- *Lead-In.* This sentence serves as your opening and transition statement to initiate the activity. You will find convenient words in quotation marks.

- *Process.* Below the header is the process. This is the step-by-step procedure to conduct the activity. Here are some of its features:

  - The steps are numbered.

  - A reminder is embedded in the script to remind you to show the slide.

  - Quotation marks are placed around statements you can make to participants.

  - This guide does not script every word you say; you are a seasoned trainer who may want to add content of your own.

  - Suggested questions to initiate group discussion are also included.

  - Notes reference anything special you should consider or remember.

  - Suggested responses are included for participant activities.

  - Some additional resource content may be included in the process steps.

  - For long activities or where time is critical, you will find time listed within parentheses.

- ◦ Instructions may also include things for you to do during the break, such as hang flipcharts on the wall.

- • *Discussion.* The facilitator will lead a large group discussion.

   Note: One feature in the materials is "In Focus," approximately half a dozen quick reminders such as Good Design ABCs or the 3Cs of a Great Trainer.

Session at a Glance

The Session at a Glance is a short overview of each module. It includes the list of activities (matching the activities listed in the Trainer's Guide—chapters 5 through 9—with the participant handout thumbnails in chapter 11). It also displays the time, the participant handout number, and any materials or equipment you may need. It is meant as a planning tool for you—not as an agenda for participants. The Session at a Glance for each module is also included in the chapter that covers that module's activities. You can also find Session at a Glance tables for all modules on the CD. From there, you may print copies to keep yourself organized during your presentation and add actual times for your particular session. Each module has its own Session at a Glance:

- • Chapter 5: Module 1—Introduction

- • Chapter 6: Module 2—Assess and Analyze

- • Chapter 7: Module 3—Design and Develop

- • Chapter 8: Module 4—Implement and Facilitate

- • Chapter 9: Module 5—Evaluate and Enhance

Time

I have intentionally omitted scheduled times on the Session at a Glance because some organizations begin their training days at 8:00 a.m. or 8:30 a.m. Some even start as early as 7:30 a.m. or as late as 9:00 a.m. My recommendation is to begin as early in the day as is feasible. It may be difficult for both you and your participants to maintain energy at 4:45 p.m. after a full day of active learning.

Breaks

The day has been scheduled so that you can allow three 10- to 15-minute breaks. The schedule allows 45 minutes for lunch. Some flexibility is built in, but you should not allow yourself to get too far behind the agenda. If you do, consider what you will need to shorten and how you will do it to make up the time.

Note: The first column of the Session at a Glance has been left blank, so you can fill in the exact times that you will start, as well as when you will take breaks and lunch. The time at the end of each day is suggested based on the material needed to cover each day. Although some flexibility exists, try to stay as close to the allotted times as possible to avoid running out of time the last day.

Session at a Glance

Table 5-1. Module 1—Introduction

ACTUAL TIME	ACTIVITY	TIME	PARTICIPANT HANDOUT	SLIDE NUMBER	MEDIA/MATERIALS
	Activity 1-1: Where's the Training Focus? Agenda Review	70 min.	1-1, 1-2	1-1 through 1-7	Markers on the tables Table tents Flipchart Index cards Sticky notes
	Activity 1-2: What Does a Trainer Do?	20 min.	1-3	1-8	
	Activity 1-3: What Is Training? The Train-the-Trainer Workshop Modules	20 min.	1-4, 1-5	1-9, 1-10	
	Activity 1-4: Focus on You— Wrap-Up of Module 1	10 min.	1-6	1-11	

Activity 1-1:	Where's the Training Focus?
	Agenda Review

Handouts 1-1, 1-2

Room Set up in pods of four to six people at each round or square table.

Materials/Equipment Participant handouts at each participant's place
Markers on the tables
One box of crayons on each table
Magnifying glasses on tables
Masking tape
Table tents
Flipchart "Focus Expectations"
Sticky notes
Welcome slide displayed as participants enter the room

Slides 1-1 through 1-7

Time 70 minutes

Lead-In "Welcome to the train-the-trainer session."

 Process

1. Introduce yourself and mention the rationale for holding the class. Refer to your needs assessment data if available.

2. Conduct a mini needs assessment to gather information about the participants. Ask them to raise their hands in response to your questions:

   - How long have they been in the training field?

     ○ Six months

     ○ One year

     ○ Two years

     ○ Two to five years

     ○ More than five years

     ○ More than 10 years

- How many have attended a train-the-trainer session in the past?

- Who designs training?

- How many believe they were destined to be a trainer?

Ask any other questions that provide you with the kind of information you would like to know about the participants. Add appropriate comments.

(5 minutes)

3. Show the "Focus on You" **slide (1-2)** and segue into the icebreaker by saying, "The theme for this train-the-trainer session is *focus*. We will focus on what works and what doesn't work in training, focus on design and delivery, focus on what's behind the scenes, and even focus on what's happening in this room. Let's take a few minutes to focus on you. Focus on what you do for fun as you introduce yourself."

Tell them to sketch a picture of what they like to focus on for fun on the back of their table tent. Suggest that they may use the crayons if they wish. Let them have about three to five minutes to draw the picture. Walk among the participants to ensure that everyone understands the task. Give a one-minute time signal before the end of the activity.

Show **slide 1-3** and ask for volunteers to begin to share:

- their names

- where they work (department or company)

- other pertinent information

- what they like to focus on for fun.

Ensure that all participants introduce themselves. Ask them to be sure their names are on their table tents. Be sure to share what you like to do when you focus on fun.

(25 minutes)

4. Show the "Where's the Training Focus" **slide (1-4)**. Hold up a magnifying glass (either one of your own or one of the inexpensive ones on the participants' tables) and tell them to turn to **handout 1-1**. State that, as trainers, we need to focus on myriad things to do our jobs. We need to focus on the organization and its need to accomplish its mission. We focus on the content we deliver to ensure that it's accurate and practical, as well as fun. We focus on ourselves to ensure that we are skilled and knowledgeable. Most important, we focus on our participants to ensure that we meet their needs as a group and as individuals. This train-the-trainer session will focus on the practical and the creative elements that will make the participants' jobs easier and their results more productive.

Let them know that they are going to explore this focus from their perspective. Ask them to move to one of the four corners of the room that corresponds to the four corners of the slide and name the corners (participants, trainer/facilitator, content, and organization). They should select their area of focus for this session. State that once a certain number (approximately one-fourth of the group size) of people are in a corner, they should go to their second choice.

Once everyone is settled, ask them to discuss what they hope to focus on in this session as it relates to training. For example, they can focus on how to design content that is fun yet practical, how I as a trainer can overcome nervousness, how to deal with disruptive participants, or how to ensure that training addresses organizational goals. State that they have 10 minutes to introduce themselves to the group, select a spokesperson, and discuss their desires.

After 10 minutes, ask each group to report what they hope to focus on in this session. List their focus expectations on a flipchart (titled "Focus Expectations") as they report to the group. Respond appropriately to each group: Confirm what will be covered, address what will not be covered, and suggest ways you can help them (recommend books, meet after the session, or locate other resources). Hang this list at the break.

(20 minutes)

5.  Tell the participants, "Now we've met each other and identified expectations. Turn to **handout 1-2** to review the agenda." Use **slides 1-5, 1-6,** and **1-7** to overview the agenda and objectives at a high level.

6. Use your favorite process to present and generate ground rules. Post the ground rules on the wall at the break.

7. Bring participants' attention to the "parking lot" on the wall. Tell them that if they have a question that is not answered immediately, they should write it on a sticky note and place it on the parking lot. Questions will be worked into the session or answered at the end. *Note:* Check any sticky notes that are added to the wall charts during breaks so that you are sure to address the questions or comments at the appropriate times. (To continue with the focus theme, you may wish to sketch a picture of binoculars, magnifying glass, or eyeglasses. You could also title it "Focus on Your Questions.")

8. Address any administrative needs, for example, location of emergency exits, bathrooms, and soda machines; whether food can be brought into the room; parking validation; or anything else that participants need to know.

Note: Remember that you are not addressing the administrative needs as the first item of the session because you are modeling the appropriate way to open your session. You may explain this during the Openings and Icebreakers activity (handouts 3-6 and 3-7) or during the first "Stop to Focus" activity (handout 2-7).

Post the flipchart pages on the wall during break.

(20 minutes)

Activity 1-2:   What Does a Trainer Do?

Handout   1-3

Materials/Equipment   None

Slides   1-8

Time   20 minutes

Lead-In   "Like any job, training can be one of the most exciting professions, but it can also have its frustrations."

Process

1. Look at **handout 1-3** with the participants. Briefly review the content at the top of the page.

2. Show **slide 1-8**; ask participants to think back to experiences they have had as a trainer and then identify frustrations and pleasures. Tell them to take three to four minutes to jot down a couple of things in the appropriate columns that caused either pleasure or frustration. Provide a time check after three minutes by saying, "Finish writing your last example and then let's get back together as a large group."

Divide the group in half. Try to have exactly the same number of people in each group. Participants stay at their tables. If you cannot divide the number of tables equally, split one in half. Ask half to discuss the frustrations and the other half to discuss the pleasures. Allow approximately seven minutes for these discussions. At the end, call time.

Ask participants to stand, take **handout 1-3** with them, and form two long lines facing each other, either at the back of the room or in a hallway. One line should be made up of those who discussed the frustrations, and the other line should be those who discussed the pleasures. Start at one end of the frustrations line and ask the first person to state one of the things the group mentioned. The person standing at the beginning of the pleasures line should say, "Yes, but . . . " and add a pleasure of training. Continue working back and forth across the two lines until you reach the end. If time permits, you may ask for additional pleasures and frustrations.

Conclude this exercise by stating that, like most jobs, training has its advantages and disadvantages. This training session, however, will help trainers learn how to turn some of their frustrations into pleasures.

Activity 1-3: What Is Training?
The Train-the-Trainer Workshop Modules

Handouts	1-4, 1-5
Materials/Equipment	None
PPT Slides	1-9, 1-10
Time	20 minutes
Lead-In	"So, what is training?"

Process

1. [handout] [PPT] Take a few ideas from the group. They will most likely all be correct. State that lots of words on **handout 1-4** describe the five phases of ADDIE, the generally accepted instructional systems design model. Use **slide 1-9** to briefly outline ADDIE.

   (5 minutes)

2. [PPT] [handout] Show **slide 1-10** and ask participants to turn to **handout 1-5**. Explain that this train-the-trainer session will follow the ADDIE model, except that it has only four modules because it combines the design and develop phases.

3. Ask the participants what percentage of their time is spent in each of the four areas listed. Listen to several comments. You can expect that the highest percentages will be in the "Design and Develop" and the "Implement and Facilitate" modules. State further that we will spend the majority of our time in these two modules.

   (10 minutes)

Activity 1-4:   Focus on You—Wrap-Up of Module 1

Handout   1-6

Materials/Equipment   None

Slides   1-11

Time   10 minutes

Lead-In   "We are wrapping up module 1. At the end of each module, you will have an opportunity to reflect on what we have discussed and capture your thoughts about what is important to you."

Process

1. Show **slide 1-11**. Tell the participants to turn to **handout 1-6** and take five to six minutes to capture their thoughts about this brief first module.

2. When you see that most people have completed their notes, give a one-minute warning and ask them to turn to module 2.

PowerPoint Slides

Ultimate
Train-the-Trainer

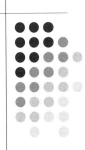

Focus on Success

Slide 1-1

Focus on You

Icebreaker:

Draw a picture on the back of your table tent that depicts what you do when you focus on fun.

Slide 1-2

Focus on You

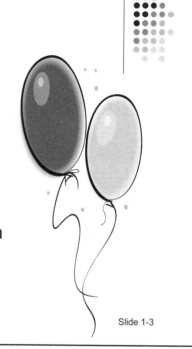

Icebreaker:

- Name
- Where you work (department or company)
- Other pertinent information you desire
- Your "fun focus"

Slide 1-3

Where's the Training Focus?

Participants   **Trainer/Facilitator**

Content   **Organization**

Slide 1-4

Agenda

Day 1	**Introduction**
	Assess and Analyze
	Design and Develop
Day 2	**Implement and Facilitate**
Day 3	**Skill Practice Delivery**
	Evaluate and Enhance
	Where Do You Go From Here?

Slide 1-5

Train-the-Trainer Objectives

- List the characteristics of an exceptional trainer.
- Discuss the phases of a training cycle.
- Conduct a training needs assessment.
- Write correct learning objectives.
- Explain what is meant by adult learning theory.
- Design a participant-centered training experience.

Slide 1-6

Train-the-Trainer Objectives

- Implement a variety of learning activities.
- Establish a positive learning environment.
- Demonstrate the appropriate use of visuals.
- Evaluate effective presentation skills.
- Name Kirkpatrick's four levels of evaluation.
- Develop an individualized development plan for yourself.

Slide 1-7

What Does a Trainer Do?

- **Pleasures**

- **Frustrations**

Slide 1-8

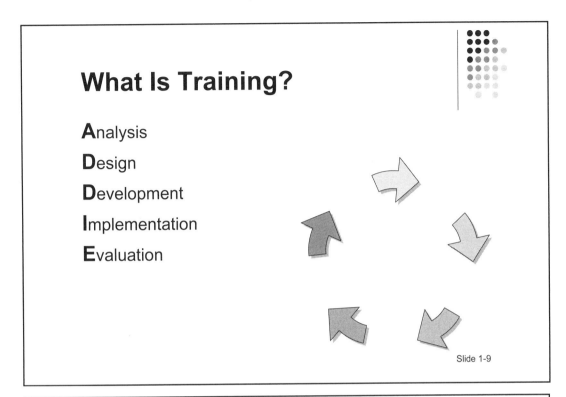

Slide 1-9

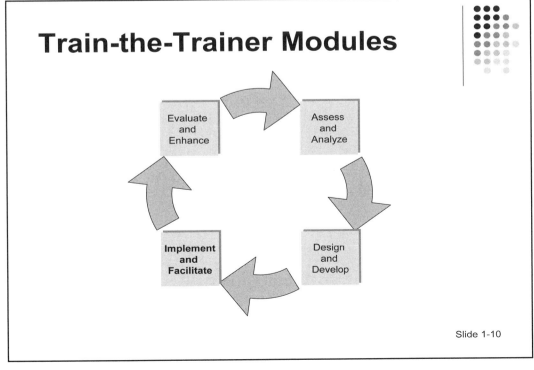

Slide 1-10

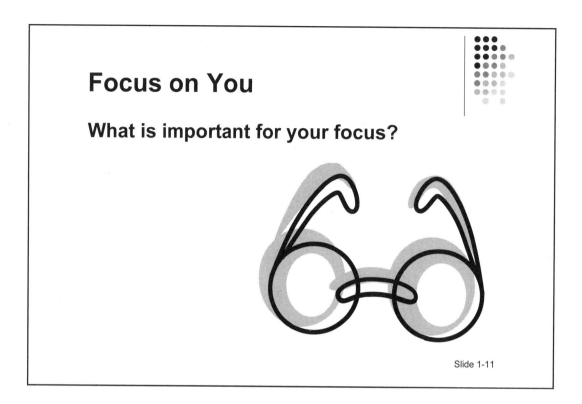

Slide 1-11

Trainer's Guide: Module 2—Assess and Analyze

6

What's in This Chapter?

- Detailed step-by-step instructions to help present the train-the-trainer activities for Module 2—Assess and Analyze

- Instructions to identify the equipment and material needs for each activity

- Instructions to determine the amount of time each activity requires

See chapter 5 for a general guide to facilitating a successful program.

Session at a Glance

Table 6-1. Module 2—Assess and Analyze

Actual Time	Activity	Time	Participant Handout	Slide Number	Media/ Materials
	Activity 2-1: Introduction to Module 2—Assess and Analyze	5 min.	2-1	2-1 through 2-5	
	Activity 2-2: Needs Assessment and Analysis Basics	10 min.	2-2	2-6, 2-7	
	Activity 2-3: How Can You Collect Data? What Questions Will You Ask? Is Training the Solution?	30 min.	2-3 to 2-5	2-8 through 2-16	
	Activity 2-4: Participant's Personal Needs Assessment	30 min.	2-6	2-17, 2-18	
	Activity 2-5: Focus on What's Happening!	15 min.	2-7	2-19	
	Activity 2-6: What Constitutes a Good Learning Objective? How Do You Write a Learning Objective? What Are Your Personal Learning Objectives?	30 min.	2-8 to 2-10	2-20 through 2-28	"Team 2 Notes" memo
	Activity 2-7: Focus on You— Wrap-Up of Module 2	15 min.	2-11	2-29	

Activity 2-1:	**Introduction to Module 2—Assess and Analyze**
Handout	2-1
Materials/Equipment	None
Slides	2-1 through 2-5
Time	5 minutes
Lead-In	"Let's begin with the Assess and Analyze module."

Process

1. Ask participants to turn to **handout 2-1**. Use **slides 2-1** through **2-5** to give an overview of the objectives for the module.

2. Refer to any objectives that are related to the list of focus expectations that you posted on the wall during the opening activity.

Activity 2-2:	**Needs Assessment and Analysis Basics**
📄 **Handout**	2-2
✖ **Materials/Equipment**	None
PPT **Slides**	2-6, 2-7
🕐 **Time**	10 minutes
💬 **Lead-In**	Show **slide 2-6** as you say: "Needs assessment and analysis are processes used to collect data to specify the problem and to determine the solution. This includes determining whether training is a solution."

🔢 Process

1. 📄 **PPT** 🗨 Continue to show **slide 2-6** and ask participants to turn to **handout 2-2**. State that we conduct needs assessments and analyze the data in almost everything we do. Ask participants for examples in their everyday life.

   Note: They may suggest big decisions, such as whether to take a trip or go back to college. These examples are correct, but encourage them to think of smaller decisions too, such as which toothpaste to purchase or whether to fill the car with gas now or later.

2. **PPT** Use **slide 2-7** to review the five steps.

3. 🕐 State that needs assessment and analysis are critical to ensure that training is as effective as possible. Refer to the bottom of the handout. Ask the participants to pair up with the person next to them to brainstorm for two minutes and think of at least one other reason to conduct a needs assessment.

4. 🗨 Ask for volunteers to share their ideas—one idea per team of two. Here are some possible reasons to conduct a needs assessment:

   - deciding whether training is the solution

   - identifying what skills to train

   - determining who needs to train.

Activity 2-3:   **How Can You Collect Data?**

What Questions Will You Ask?

Is Training the Solution?

📄 **Handouts**   2-3 through 2-5

✖ **Materials/Equipment**   None

PPT **Slides**   2-8 through 2-16

🕐 **Time**   30 minutes

💬 **Lead-In**   "The most important aspect of a needs assessment is collecting data."

🔢 **Process**

1. 📄 PPT 🕐 Ask participants to turn to **handout 2-3**. State that data can be collected in many ways and that seven methods are listed here. Use **slides 2-8** through **2-14** to briefly describe each method, but do not share advantages or disadvantages.
   Assign a method to pairs of participants; ask them to identify the advantages and disadvantages. Allow about three to four minutes. Process the page as a large group. Suggest that everyone fill in the spaces as teams report on their method. Here are some possible responses:

   - Interviews are a beneficial method when used early; they can help clarify or pinpoint the problem. The best participants to interview are those who express themselves well in person. The disadvantage of the interview is that it's time consuming.

   - Focus groups use a precise process that comes out of the marketing field, where the same questions are asked and information is recorded. Two advantages are that you can interview more people in a shorter period of time and the group members can react to each others' ideas. The disadvantage of a focus group is that a quiet person may defer to the others and may not contribute much.

   - Questionnaires are a good way to reach a large or geographically dispersed population in a limited period of time, and they are a comparatively inexpensive way to collect data. One drawback is that it is one-way communication and does not allow for free expression, so you may miss some critical data points. Return rates are often low, and the questions need to be tested for clarity before you send them to people.

- Observations are a good way to collect data if you need direct contact with the situation, for example, if you need to assess the job site and how individuals interact on the job. It may, however, be difficult to record data and be time consuming. In addition, observations are only indications of behavior and don't explain the reason behind the data.

- Performance data reviews can be an unobtrusive way to identify trouble spots, although it may be a time-consuming method that requires the reviewer to have specialized content analysis skills. The data may be confounded by unseen variables, such as equipment downtime or external expectations.

- Informal discussions are a good way to begin to shape the data collection, especially if you have limited information about the problem, but the discussions must be followed up with a more structured approach. You may get a candid opinion, but it may also be biased.

- Knowledge tests are a way to gather information, although individuals may have the knowledge but be unable to apply it. Because the test measures knowledge, attitude is not mixed into the response. A knowledge test, however, does not measure the actual skills that may or may not be used on the job.

🕐 (15 minutes)

2. **PPT**   Point out that **handout 2-4** (two pages) is a resource that provides a list of questions that one might include in a needs assessment. Show **slide 2-15** and lead a large group discussion about why these are good questions. Here are some suggested responses:

Why

- 👂 It helps the person to focus on the problem rather than the solution ("I want training in teamwork").

- It identifies symptoms and causes, which helps focus on the situation, to determine whether it is a training problem.

- It focuses on the organizational aspects to ensure that you will be able to enlist business support for the training.

- The last question forces the individual to specify the outcome—the trainer's objectives.

Who

- These questions provide you with a clear understanding of who the participants will be and the dilemma they may have.

- Questions about the experts may lead you to the subject matter experts (SMEs).

- Questions about the disadvantages may uncover a situation that training cannot solve, which would lead you to determine whether this really is a problem with a training solution.

What

- Learn more about the available training (on site or off the shelf), what training the audience has had, and where the problem exists to help you determine other available solutions (other than you and your department).

- Ask for other solutions to help get at the root cause; you may realize that training may not be the right solution.

- Ask what happens if training is not provided; it may prove that the solution is more expensive than the problem, so it may be better to do nothing.

Where

- These are questions of logistics, but it is important to discuss them early.

When

- This may reveal what is driving the timeframe, for example, a boss said, "Do it now or else . . ." or a government regulation requires completion in a timely manner.

- Longevity gives you an indication of the maintenance that might be required (how often you need to revise and update the material).

- This question indicates whether the turnaround will be tight.

- This provides information about how the assessment fits into your department's schedule.

How

- These questions, by focusing on money, clarify that training has a cost.

- Before beginning, you need to know who will support the training with resources.

- The training will be successful only if participants are able to transfer the knowledge to their workplace, and this is the best time to learn this.

For additional content, see "The 60-Minute Needs Analysis" by Nanette Miner in the *2009 Pfeiffer Annual: Training* (Biech, 2009).

 (15 minutes)

3. As you wrap up **handout 2-4**, point out the camera graphic at the bottom of the second page. State that participants will find this "In Focus" graphic throughout their materials. The purpose is to *focus* on several key points that will help them remember the most important aspects of a segment of the train the trainer. In this case, it is to remember the "Six Needs Assessment Questions": why, who, what, where, when, and how.

4. [PPT] [ ] Show **slide 2-16** and point out that **handout 2-5** is a reminder that a critical step during the needs assessment process is to consider whether the problem really can be solved with training. Suggest that participants review the questions on this page before they begin their next training design.

| **Activity 2-4:** | **Participant's Personal Needs Assessment** |

| 🗎 **Handout** | 2-6 |

| ⚒ **Materials/Equipment** | None |

| 📊 **Slides** | 2-17, 2-18 |

| ⏰ **Time** | 30 minutes |

| 🗩 **Lead-In** | "We spent several minutes discussing assessments; let's give you an opportunity to do your own self-assessment." |

🔢 Process

1. 🗎 📊 Have participants turn to **handout 2-6** (three pages) as you display **slide 2-17**. Tell them that they should take about 15 minutes to complete the assessment. They will not share their scores with anyone, so they should be completely honest with themselves. ⏰ Give a time signal after approximately seven minutes, stating that they should be about half finished. Give another signal about two minutes before the end; if it appears that many are not nearing completion, ask how much time they need to finish.

    Walk around and watch for anyone who may be having difficulty.

2. Ask the participants to total their scores. Ask them what they are thinking after completing the self-assessment. Take several comments.

3. Tell the participants that they should pay particular attention to three things:

   • First, the items for which they received the highest score. They will become their strengths from which to build, and the participants should list those where indicated.

   • Second, the participants may want to place a check next to the two or three items rated the lowest in the last column. The negative numbers indicate that the importance on the job is greater than their ability, so these are items they need to focus on first.

   • Third, their overall score. The maximum score totaled in the first column is 150.

4. 📊 Use **slide 2-18** to explain the total score:
   150 = Perfect Score
   120 = Proficient
   110 = Above Average
   85 = Average

Explain that although the score reflects skills at a point in time, it is not the most important aspect of this assessment. The participants have identified areas that need improvement and areas in which they are skilled, and they have a chance to improve specific skills during this session. Allow time for them to record their personal information on the last page (talents and development needs).

Activity 2-5:	**Focus on What's Happening!**
Handout	2-7
Materials/Equipment	None
Slides	2-19
Time	15 minutes
Lead-In	"What have we done so far?"

Process

1. Display **slide 2-19** and have participants turn to **handout 2-7**. State, "We are living what you are learning. Every so often during this training session, we will stop everything we are doing to *focus* on what we have experienced through another lens. You have been observing this session through a participant's eyes. Now try to examine this session through the designer's eyes. Use a magnifying glass and consider all the details that have gone into the design. Think about what has been happening in the room from the designer's perspective. What have you noticed?"

   "This is also a time to discuss questions about the process. If I have done something that I wish I had done differently, I will tell you that, as well. So, rise above the session for a different perspective, look down on our first couple of hours, and *focus* on what we have done so far. Use the magnifying glass on your tables and look carefully at the details of this session."

2. As participants share their ideas, listen carefully. If explanations are required, give them. Answer questions where necessary. Share any errors you have made and tell participants how you intend to do it differently next time.

   Note: Take care not to become defensive.

3. You should expect to hear: Trainer started on time; used humor; tied the icebreaker to content; used variety of activities; tried different groupings; built rapport by making eye contact, using names, nodding, and affirming comments; ensured that everyone spoke; did not request anyone to share poor scores; discussed expectations; and gave time milestones.

   Note: If you have not discussed why the logistics were placed about an hour into the session, this would be a good discussion starter.

Note: Allow plenty of time for participants to speak up; which means you may have to stop talking and listen. If you need some questions to encourage conversation, however, you may use the ones on the handout, as well as those listed here.

It's time to stop what you are doing and focus on the training techniques that have been modeled.

- What trainer/facilitator skills have you observed?

- What design aspects have been incorporated?

- How has the trainer made the room conducive to learning?

- Which techniques work?

- Which techniques don't work?

- What would you be doing right now if you were the trainer?

Activity 2-6:   What Constitutes a Good Learning Objective?

How Do You Write a Learning Objective?

What Are Your Personal Learning Objectives?

Handouts	2-8 through 2-10
Materials/Equipment	Copies of the "Team 2 Notes" memo for activity 2-6 (on the CD) that says, "Do not reveal these instructions to the other team. When the facilitator says 'Start,' in less than 1 minute, pass the marker around so that everyone on your team touches it without speaking. The last person to touch the marker goes to the flipchart and writes, 'Team 2—Tried and True!'"
Slides	2-20 through 2-28
Time	30 minutes
Lead-In	"Learning objectives are written to specify the desired performance (knowledge or skill) once the training has been completed."

 Process

1. State, "Before we begin this section, I'd like you to participate in a game. I will divide you into two teams, and I'll keep time." Divide the participants into two teams based on where they are sitting. Assign one team to be Team 1 and the other to be Team 2. Give a marker to the person on Team 1 who is sitting closest to the flipchart. Say, "Start!" Do not say anything else. Expect everyone to be flustered and not know what they should be doing. Observe the time on your watch (or another clock) intently. After 60 seconds, call out, "Time!"

   State, "Now it's Team 2's turn." Distribute the "Team 2 Notes" memo for activity 2-6 to the team members and give them time to read it. Hand them the marker and say, "Start!" At the end of 60 seconds say, "Time!" and declare Team 2 to be the winner. After the laughter subsides, ask each of the teams, "How did you feel about the game?" Ask, "Why is there a difference of opinion between Team 1 and Team 2?" State, "Oh, you mean it is easy to win when you know what to do?" Make the connections between this silly game and a well-written learning objective that is specific, measurable, attainable, relevant, and time bound.

2. Ask a rhetorical question, "So did this game show us the importance of learning objectives?" After you receive several responses, ask participants how many are familiar with the SMART objective acronym. Show **slides 2-20** through **2-24** and state what each of the letters stands for. Although the instructions for the game were not an objective, they did incorporate the SMART characteristics. A SMART objective tells the participant what to do, just as the instructions told Team 2 what to do. Ask participants to turn to **handout 2-8**.

3. If you need to share more information, use the slides to explain what constitutes a good objective based on the SMART acronym:

   - *S*pecific: You can see it; ask for action words that you can see (for example: name, complete, demonstrate) and words you cannot see (for example: understand, believe).

   - *M*easurable: It can be counted, assigned a percentage, or answered with a yes or no.

   - *A*ttainable: It should be a stretch, but not impossible.

   - *R*elevant: It should be related to an organizational goal and appropriate for the training session.

   - *T*ime-bound: It should be associated with a date or a time frame, for example, by the end of the session.

 (5 minutes)

4. Ask participants to turn to **handout 2-9** and use **slides 2-25** through **2-28** to present the formula for writing an objective: "*Who* will do *what*, by *when*, and *how well*?"
   Discuss the ABCD model of a good objective:

   - *A*udience (who)

   - *B*ehavior (will do what)

   - *C*ondition (by when, with what assistance)

   - *D*egree (how well).

5. Ask participants to form small groups based on their birthdays: Quarters 1, 2, 3, and 4. Tell them to examine the four objectives presented in **handout 2-9** and to determine which objectives are complete.
   A review of each objective should include these comments:
   (1) Missing C and D. In addition, B is not measurable or observable. You cannot tell if someone really understands.
   (2) Missing C. It can sometimes be accepted that no assistance is given; however, objective should still include *when*.
   (3) Although D is missing, it can sometimes be accepted that 100 percent is intended.
   (4) Although not in the same sequence, all components are there.

   Note: If you are short on time, don't move into different groups and assign only one objective to each table.

 (10 minutes)

6. Ask participants to turn to **handout 2-10**. Using the results of their self-assessments on **handout 2-6**, ask them to write three objectives for themselves for this session.

7. Participants who finish early can evaluate each of their objectives using the SMART chart at the bottom of **handout 2-10**.

8. Ask for a few examples. Facilitate discussion around the examples.

(15 minutes)

Activity 2-7:   Focus on You—Wrap-Up of Module 2

Handout   2-11

Materials/Equipment   None

Slides   2-29

Time   15 minutes

Lead-In   "We are wrapping up module 2."

Process

1. Show **slide 2-29** and tell the participants to turn to **handout 2-11** to capture their thoughts about this module.

2. When you see that most people have completed their notes, give a one-minute warning and ask them to turn to module 3.

PowerPoint Slides

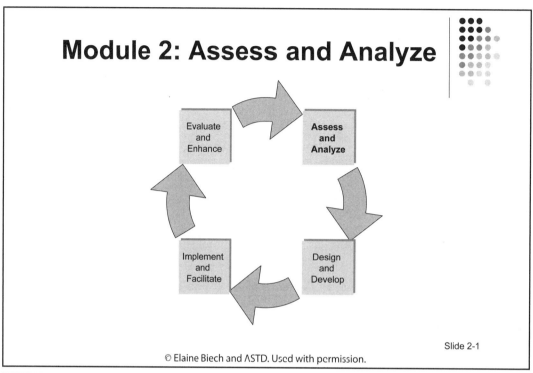

Module 2: Assess and Analyze

Slide 2-1

© Elaine Biech and ASTD. Used with permission.

Module 2 Objectives

- **Explain the fundamentals of conducting a needs analysis.**

Slide 2-2

Module 2 Objectives

- Explain the fundamentals of conducting a needs analysis.
- **Identify questions used in a needs assessment.**

Slide 2-3

Module 2 Objectives

- Explain the fundamentals of conducting a needs analysis.
- Identify questions used in a needs assessment.
- **Assess your personal development needs.**

Slide 2-4

Module 2 Objectives

- Explain the fundamentals of conducting a needs analysis.
- Identify questions used in a needs assessment
- Assess your personal development needs.
- **Develop correct learning objectives.**

Slide 2-5

What Is a Needs Assessment?

Needs assessment and analysis are data collection processes used to specify problems and to determine solutions.

Slide 2-6

Needs Assessment Steps

- Identify a need.

- Determine a plan.

- Gather the data.

- Analyze the data.

- Make a decision.

Slide 2-7

How to Collect Data?

- **Interviews**

Slide 2-8

How to Collect Data?

- Interviews

- **Focus Groups**

Slide 2-9

How to Collect Data?

- Interviews

- Focus Groups

- **Questionnaires**

Slide 2-10

How to Collect Data?

- Interviews

- Focus Groups

- Questionnaires

- **Observations**

Slide 2-11

How to Collect Data?

- Interviews

- Focus Groups

- Questionnaires

- Observations

- **Performance Data Reviews**

Slide 2-12

How to Collect Data?

- Interviews

- Focus Groups

- Questionnaires

- Observations

- Performance Data Reviews

- **Informal Discussions**

Slide 2-13

How to Collect Data?

- Interviews

- Focus Groups

- Questionnaires

- Observations

- Performance Data Reviews

- Informal Discussions

- **Knowledge Tests**

Slide 2-14

What Questions Will You Ask?

How do the answers
to these questions
help you make decisions?

Slide 2-15

Is Training the Solution?

Slide 2-16

Participant's Personal
Needs Assessment

Slide 2-17

Participant's Self-Assessment

150 = Perfect Score

120 = Proficient

110 = Above Average

 85 = Average

Slide 2-18

Focus on What's Happening!

- Examine this train-the-trainer session through another lens:

  - What training techniques have you noticed?

  - What have you experienced?

  - What have you observed?

Slide 2-19

What Constitutes a Good Objective?

- **S**pecific

Slide 2-20

What Constitutes a Good Objective?

- **S**pecific
- **M**easurable

Slide 2-21

What Constitutes a Good Objective?

- **S**pecific
- **M**easurable
- **A**ttainable, yet a stretch

Slide 2-22

What Constitutes a Good Objective?

- **S**pecific
- **M**easurable
- **A**ttainable, yet a stretch
- **R**elevant

Slide 2-23

What Constitutes a Good Objective?

- **S**pecific
- **M**easurable
- **A**ttainable, yet a stretch
- **R**elevant
- **T**ime-bound

Slide 2-24

Learning Objectives

- *Who*

Slide 2-25

Learning Objectives

- *Who* will *do what,*

Slide 2-26

Learning Objectives

- *Who* will *do what,* by *when,*

Slide 2-27

Learning Objectives

- *Who* will *do what,* by *when,* and *how well*.

Slide 2-28

Focus on You

What is important for your focus?

Slide 2-29

Trainer's Guide: Module 3—Design and Develop

7

What's in This Chapter?

- Detailed step-by-step instructions to help present the train-the-trainer activities for Module 3—Design and Develop

- Instructions to identify the equipment and material needs for each activity

- Instructions to determine the amount of time each activity requires

See chapter 5 for a general guide to facilitating a successful program.

▲　　▲　　▲

Session at a Glance

Table 7-1. Module 3—Design and Develop

Actual Time	Activity	Time	Participant Handout	Slide Number	Media/Materials
	Activity 3-1: Introduction to Module 3—Design and Develop	5 min.	3-1	3-1 through 3-6	
	Activity 3-2: Introducing Design and Adult Learning Principles Malcolm Knowles and Adult Learning Principles Adult Learning—Answer Their Questions	45 min.	3-2 to 3-4	3-7 through 3-14	Flipchart Pairwise card set
	Activity 3-3: Six Recommendations for Effective Training Design	30 min.	3-5	3-15	
	Activity 3-4: FOCUS Your Openings for Added Value What's an Icebreaker?	20 min.	3-6, 3-7	3-16 through 3-17	
	Activity 3-5: Focus on What's Happening! Closing	20 min.	3-8	3-18	
	End Day 1				
	Activity 3-6: Day 2 Open	15 min.			
	Activity 3-7: Activities—Countless Alternatives to Lecture	40 min.	3-9	3-19	Team prizes such as a bag of popcorn or M&Ms

continued on next page

Table 7-1. Module 3—Design and Develop, *continued*

Actual Time	Activity	Time	Participant Handout	Slide Number	Media/ Materials
	Activity 3-8: Using KSAs for Instructional Design Selecting Activities Based on the KSA	25 min.	3-10, 3-11	3-20	
	Activity 3-9: Developing Training Support Materials—Visuals	15 min.	3-12	3-21	
	Activity 3-10: Know Your Training Style Training Style Self-Assessment Training Style Self-Assessment Scoring Pulling It All Together Understand Your Training Style	45 min.	3-13 to 3-17	3-22 through 3-29	
	Activity 3-11: Help! I've Been Asked to Conduct a Webinar! Focus on You— Wrap-Up of Module 3	15 min.	3-18, 3-19	3-30	

Activity 3-1:   Introduction to Module 3—Design and Develop

Handout   3-1

Materials/Equipment   None

Slides   3-1 through 3-6

Time   5 minutes

Lead-In   "Let's turn to the Design and Develop module and review the objectives."

Process

1.   Ask participants to turn to **handout 3-1**. Use **slides 3-1** through **3-6** to provide an overview of the objectives for the module.

2.   Refer to any objectives that are related to the list of focus expectations that you posted on the wall during the opening activity.

3.   Darken the PowerPoint projection.

Activity 3-2:	**Introducing Design and Adult Learning Principles**
	Malcolm Knowles and Adult Learning Principles
	Adult Learning—Answer Their Questions

📄	**Handouts**	3-2 through 3-4
✖	**Materials/Equipment**	Pairwise card set from the CD
⊙		Two prepared flipcharts labeled "Learner-Focused" and "Training-Focused"
PPT	**Slides**	3-7 through 3-14
🕐	**Time**	45 minutes
🗩	**Lead-In**	"Let's consider the skill sets required of a designer."

🔢 Process

1. 📄 Ask participants to turn to **handout 3-2**. Provide an overview of the skill sets required of a training designer. Note the last one, which is to understand adult learning principles.

2. PPT Show **slide 3-7** and say, "Let's begin this module by exploring adult learning principles. Think of three things you have learned in the past two months and why you learned them. List them on your page."

🕐 (5 minutes)

3. 🗩 Ask for several examples. Repeat them, highlighting that in each case, the participants either wanted to learn or needed to learn. Point out that adults learn in a different way from children, who generally learn something in school to learn something new. Each of us learned to count to 10 so that in first grade we could learn to add, so that in second grade we could learn to subtract, so that in third grade we could learn our multiplication tables, so that in junior high we could learn algebra, so that in high school we could learn trigonometry and calculus. This is unlike the examples we just had where we learn to change a tire because we have to or we learn to play piano because we want to.

🕐 (10 minutes)

4. Ask participants to summarize what they discovered on the bottom of the page. Suggest that they use the "In Focus" graphic to think about the important aspects of training design that come next.

They include "Good Design ABCs," as well as suggestions to get participant's *attention*, to help them practice the *behaviors*, and finally to give them the *confidence* to use what they have learned.

5. ☐ PPT Ask the participants to turn to **handout 3-3**. Use **slide 3-7** to present a brief lecture about the six adult learning principles. Content begins in the next paragraph. Throughout the discussion, ask for examples; ask why this might be true; ask if this is really so different from the way children learn; and interject a true-false question, or other questions to encourage interaction.

Lecturette: Knowles Believed That

- PPT 🔊 *Slide 3-8*. Adults need to know why they should learn something before they invest time in a learning event. As trainers, we must ensure that the learners know the purpose for training as early as possible. Knowles believed that the first task of the facilitator was to help learners be aware of their need to know the content. This is similar to Bob Pike's radio station, WII-FM, an abbreviation of "what's in it for me." Participants want to know if they will use this information on the job, if it will be required, if it will make their job easier, if it will actually jeopardize their jobs because the organization may not need as many people, and if they will have to change something to add this to their repertoire. Basically, participants need to know how this information and content is going to affect them and why they should care.

- PPT 🔊 *Slide 3-9*. Adults enter any learning situation with a self-concept of themselves as self-directing, responsible grown-ups. Therefore, as trainers, we must help adults identify their needs and direct their own learning experience. Participants come into the training session with a great deal of responsibility and the knowledge that they may lose something by walking into the classroom. Some are afraid that they might lose their freedom to act as adults. Some believe this as a result of their strong memories of grade school when they were under someone else's direction.

- PPT 🔊 *Slide 3-10*. Adults come to a learning opportunity with a wealth of experience and a great deal to contribute. Trainers will be more successful if they identify ways to build on and make use of adults' hard-earned experience. When trainers link new material to learners' existing knowledge, they create an influential and relevant learning experience for participants. If some participants already know the information, trainers need to tap into that knowledge and use participants to expound on the concepts for others. If too many learners know the content, trainers must question the needs assessment process. However, sometimes trainers need to deliver content that contradicts what participants currently know. In those cases, trainers must help participants remove or change the old concept to make room for the new one. Participants also bring their habits and biases into the session; they have a wide variety of different experiences, which makes it impossible to design a one-size-fits-all training program.

- PPT 🔊 *Slide 3-11*. Adults have a strong readiness to learn those things that will help them effectively cope with daily life. Adults view training that directly relates to situations they face as more relevant. Training should be scheduled as close as possible to the time the new skills and knowledge will be required; for example, training participants to use new software several weeks before the software is installed is pointless.

- PPT 🐭 *Slide 3-12.* Adults are willing to devote energy to learning those things that they believe will help them perform a task or solve a problem. Trainers who determine needs and interests, and develop content in response to these needs, will be most helpful to adult learners. Find ways to continue to relate the training to real life. Participants will learn new information and new skills if they want or need to learn it. Although adults are willing to devote energy, few are comfortable sitting for too long; be sure to take breaks so they can talk with other participants and be rejuvenated.

- PPT 🐭 *Slide 3-13.* Adults are more responsive to internal motivators, such as increased self-esteem, than to external motivators, such as higher salaries. When trainers create a safe learning environment, they ensure that this internal motivation is not blocked by barriers, such as a poor self-concept or time constraints. Trainers must also be aware of situations that may inhibit participants' motivation to learn, including fear of failure or the inability to deal with change positively. A good trainer tries to identify what motivates each participant.

6. Tell the participants to work in pairs for the next brief activity. Pass out the learner-focused/ training-focused pairwise card set, so that each person has one, and ask the participants to find their partners. Half of the cards contain things trainers would do if they were focused on the learner, and the other half contains things they would do if they were focused only on getting the training done.

Note: You will copy a set and cut them apart. You may wish to put them in a paper bag or box for people to draw one out. There are 22 cards, so if you have more than 22 in your session, you will need to add extra pairs for the additional people.

7. 📄 PPT Ask each pair of participants to turn to **handout 3-4.** Show **slide 3-14,** and tell them that theory and principles are great, but knowing how to apply the information is more important. Assign each pair one of the adult learning principles and tell them they have about 10 minutes to identify how they would incorporate it into the design and in the delivery. Ask for volunteers to report on their ideas.

Possible Responses

(1) **"Why do I need to know this?"** Adults need to know why they should learn something before investing time in a learning event.

Design

- Plan time at the beginning of the course to address the purpose of the session.

- Build in time to respond to questions about the need to know.

- Be prepared to respond to questions about the organization's ulterior motives.

- Ensure that the objectives are clear and directed at what the participants will learn.

- Decide whether a listing of expectations is required for the session.

- Design a self-evaluation.

Delivery

- Write the purpose on a flipchart page and post it on the wall.

- Give participants time to vent if necessary.

- Be prepared to respond to comments such as, "My boss should be here."

- Link the content to the participants' jobs and particular issues they may face.

(2) **"Will I be able to make some decisions, or are you going to re-create my grade school experience?"** Adults enter any learning situation with a self-concept of themselves as self-directing, responsible grown-ups.

Design

- If a self-assessment has been designed, be sure to allow time for participants to process their results by themselves or in a small, safe group.

- Avoid materials that use words reminiscent of school. Do not use any words that remind participants of their school experience, such as students, teachers, workbooks, lessons, education, report card, grade, test, desk, and classroom.

- Design a "bright ideas" board where participants can post ideas or names of books that can help other participants with their unique concerns.

Delivery

- Welcome participants with a warm greeting and a cup of coffee.

- Announce that participants can get up, move around, get a cup of coffee, or get anything else that will make them comfortable.

- Emphasize that you encourage all questions.

- Allow participants to establish their own ground rules.

(3) **"Why am I here? Why is she here? What do they think they can teach me?"** Adults come to a learning opportunity with a wealth of experience and a great deal to contribute.

Design

- Interview participants before you design the session to identify typical participant expertise and experience.

- If something has changed, identify ways to allow participants to let go of the old and welcome the new. Sometimes, journaling or self-guided questions address this concern.

- Build in time for discussion.

- Design an icebreaker that allows participants to get to know each other and what each has to contribute.

Delivery

- Allow participants to add to the learning objectives.

- Use teach-backs as one learning method.

- Allow for differences of opinion.

- If everyone in the session understands the content, speed up. If most do not understand, repeat the portion. If some know it and some don't, find ways to tap into the expertise in the room that will be beneficial to everyone.

(4) **"How is this going to simplify my life? How will this make my job easier?"** Adults have a strong readiness to learn those things that will help them cope effectively with daily life.

Design

- Address issues that participants face on the job.

- Develop case studies, critical incidents, and role plays that focus on real daily work issues.

- Interview participants before you design to obtain specific examples.

Delivery

- Allow time for participants to ask questions about implementation back on the job.

- Make yourself available at the breaks, at lunch, and after the session to discuss unique situations with individuals.

- Establish your own credibility without bragging and combine it with an I-want-to-help-you attitude.

(5) **"Do I want to learn this? Do I need to learn this?"** Adults are willing to devote energy to learning those things that they believe will help them perform a task or solve a problem.

Design

- Build in a problem-solving clinic where participants bring up their own problems that they need to solve.

- Allow time in the design for self-reflection so participants can revise their thought processes or adapt the material to their own situations.

- Design experiential learning scenarios that link the material to the reason a participant might either want or need to invest the time to learn the content.

Delivery

- Use yourself as an example to share why you wanted or needed to learn the information.

- Use a "parking lot" flipchart to encourage participants to post their questions and add ideas.

(6) **"Why would I want to learn this? Am I open to this information and, if not, why not?"** Adults are more responsive to internal motivators, such as increased self-esteem, than to external motivators, such as higher salaries.

Design

- Plan activities that help participants explore their own motivation; journaling or small group discussions may be useful.

- Participants can be intrinsically motivated if they know how they fit into the bigger plan from the organization's viewpoint.

- Find ways for participants to explore their personal growth and development needs.

Delivery

- Create a safe learning climate that allows participants to be themselves.

- Get to know all participants during some one-on-one time.

    (30 minutes)

8   To close the session, have the participants post their pairwise cards on the correct flipchart page, which you have posted at the back of the room.

| Activity 3-3: | Six Recommendations for Effective Training Design |

| **Handout** | 3-5 |

| **Materials/Equipment** | None |

| **Slides** | 3-15 |

| **Time** | 30 minutes |

| **Lead-In** | "We've all attended training programs that have been very good and then some that have not been so good. What made the difference?" |

Process

1. Take several comments and state that less-than-stellar training programs often may result from either a flaw in the design or a lack of preparation, rather than the training delivery itself. Ask for the participants' thoughts.

2. Ask participants to turn to **handout 3-5**. Review the content using **slide 3-15** to guide you. State that the bottom half of the page includes a list of important design elements.

    Ask them to grade the 11 design elements for the train-the-trainer session so far, using a school grading system of A, B, C, D, or F. Allow about five minutes. State that they can add a word or two to explain why they graded it the way they did. When everyone (or almost everyone) has completed the grading, ask them to form groups, each including one person from each table.

    Tell the participants to find a place to sit and discuss their grades and their rationale. Watch the time, allowing about 10 minutes for the discussion. You may want some groups to start at the top and work down and others to start at the bottom and work up. Lead a large group discussion about their comments. If grades are low, ask what they would do to change the design

3. State that a template similar to the one on the next page of the handout can be used to organize a design. Ask the participants to identify the features of the template that make it useful during the design process.

Possible Responses

Here are some responses you can expect:

- Time is listed for each activity; it helps to know during what part of the day you are working.

- Listing learning methods ensures a variety of small/large group, active/quiet, reflection/involved, and other various method characteristics.

- Objectives are kept in front of the designer.

- Place to record materials or media is required.

- Pages help create the agenda later.

4. Summarize by stating that you may start your design with the opening and icebreaker. Let's consider next what the design should include in the opening.

Activity 3-4:	**FOCUS Your Openings for Added Value**
	What's an Icebreaker?

📄	**Handout**	3-6, 3-7
✖	**Materials/Equipment**	None
PPT	**Slides**	3-16, 3-17
🕐	**Time**	20 minutes
🗩	**Lead-In**	"First impressions are critical. A good trainer will catch and hold participants' attention right from the start."

 Process

1. 🎯 Ask the participants, "What do you want to accomplish during the opening of your session?"

2. 📄 PPT After several responses, ask participants to turn to **handout 3-6**. Using **slide 3-16** and your own words, briefly explain the FOCUS acronym:

   - *F*acilitate interest and participation.

   - *O*ffer something about yourself.

   - *C*larify expectations.

   - *U*nderstand participant needs.

   - *S*tate the ground rules.

3. PPT 🕐 Divide participants into five groups. Show **slide 3-17**. You may wish to break the participants up into five groups based on the color of the marker they used to write their names on their table tents, provided that each table had at least five different colors of markers at each table. (You can do this during your planning and room setup.) Once they are in their five groups, assign one of the five things you need to accomplish during an opening to each group. Tell them that this is a five-in-five activity. Give them five minutes to identify five ideas that could be added to the page in their category. For example, two ways to facilitate interest and participation could be to ask for ideas or tell a funny story. An example of a way to understand participants' needs is to form small groups to create a list of the participants' needs.

4. Ask each group to report back. Suggest that participants may want to add these ideas to their pages. After their reports, ask the participants, "What do these results say about you as trainers?" Anticipate responses such as, "we have ideas," or "there is much experience in the room." Then ask, "So what does this say about your participants?" Expect to facilitate a brief discussion about the wealth of knowledge in any training session and how important it is to allow participants to contribute ideas.

5. Summarize by asking how the opening earlier in the day provided FOCUS.

6. Options based on your time: **handout 3-7** can be a resource that requires only a brief mention, or it could be an introduction to the question listed at the bottom, "What's the most creative or effective icebreaker you know about?"

Activity 3-5:   **Focus on What's Happening!**

Handout   3-8

Materials/Equipment   Index cards

Slides   3-18

Time   20 minutes

Lead-In   "Time to stop and focus on what's happening in the session again."

Process

1. Show **slide 3-18**. Tell the participants, "Once again, let's stop everything we are doing and *focus* on what we have experienced through another lens. We have just started the design phase, so think about this session through the designer's eyes. Use a magnifying glass and consider all the details that have gone into the design. What have you noticed?"

2. As participants share their ideas, listen carefully. Suggest that they may wish to take notes on **handout 3-8**. If explanations are required, give them. Answer questions where necessary. Share any errors you have made and tell participants how you intend to do it differently next time. Expect more questions this time.

   Note: Take care not to become defensive.

3. You should expect to hear: varied the way we formed groups, kept us moving around in the afternoon, encouraged participation during a lecturette, used acronyms to remember key concepts, used various ways to summarize, planned transitions, prepared well, took time during break to answer questions, addressed low energy, increased the risk level, and all the other things you are doing right!

4. This is likely the end of Day 1. It is an excellent way to end the day. If so, complete the following step.

5. Wrap-Up for the Day:

   - Ask participants to find one person in the room and share the most interesting thing they learned during the day.

   - Ask participants to rate the day using an index card, on a scale of 1–7 (1 is low; 7 is high). Tell them to add one statement about why they rated the day as they did.

   Note: You will compile these scores after participants leave and create a graph on a flipchart page. Share the results with the participants at the beginning of Day 2.

Activity 3-6:   Open Day 2

📄 Handout

None

✖ Materials/Equipment

Flipchart with the graphic results of the Wrap-Up, in which participants rated Day 1 on a scale of 1–7.

PPT Slides

None

🕐 Time

15 minutes

💬 Lead-In

"How was your evening?"

🔢 Process

1. Tell the participants, "Welcome back."

2. Check in with them about the following:

   • How are we doing on the ground rules?

   • Is there anything to add about the expectations?

   • What questions do you have about the content that we covered yesterday?

3. Share the results from the index card evaluation the evening before.

   • Reveal the scores on the flipchart.

   • Read a few comments that support the numbers.

   • Facilitate discussion about the results and ask what they might do if they had received the same results.

4. State that it is time to return to the content and ask if they can remember what you were discussing the day before (design and develop).

Activity 3-7:   Activities—Countless Alternatives to Lecture

Handout   3-9

Materials/Equipment   Prizes for each table (for example, a bag of popcorn, M&Ms, or bubble gum)

Slides   3-19

Time   40 minutes

Lead-In   "How many of you have designed a training program?"

Process

1. Say, "If you have designed a training program, you know how much work it is and how many things there are to think about. This session does not cover enough to make you an instructional designer, but we will discuss at least enough information to ensure that you know a good training design when you see one and that you will be able to troubleshoot a design that is not working." Ask them where they start with a design. The correct answer is with the objectives.

2. Ask participants to turn to **handout 3-9** and state that while there are dozens of things to remember during design, the one that often makes or breaks a training session is the variety of learning methods that might be included in the design. The more variety, the easier it is for participants to remain engaged. There are hundreds of alternative learning methods you can use.

   A well-constructed activity enhances learning because the participant experiences the learning by being personally involved. For example, in the classic NASA "Lost on the Moon" exercise, participants experience the power and value of group decision making.

 (10 minutes)

 Ask, "Why would you use an activity anyway?" Anticipate these responses and others:

- Activities are energizing.

- Games give people a break, let them stretch (their brains, as well as their bodies), relieve stress, and help them get energized.

- Activities get people working together.

- Activities build rapport among participants to increase the amount of knowledge floating around the room.

- More learning occurs when everyone shares and learns from each other.

Note: This is a good time to make the point that as a trainer/facilitator you have a body of knowledge, but the combined knowledge of your group far outweighs what you know.

- Activities promote learning by doing. Participants will retain the knowledge better if you can engage as many of their senses as possible.

- Activities provide you with a way to reinforce information. It would be pretty boring if you stated the same things over and over in the same way, even though we know that repetition is good.

- Activities are motivational. Learners respond because they are actively involved. It is a pleasant way to learn.

Note: Thousands of activities, games, and exercises exist; you can also create your own. One of the best resources for games is the *Games Trainers Play* series by Ed Scannell and John Newstrom (Scannell and Newstrom, 1983–1998). The best resource for experiential learning activities (ELAs) is the *Pfeiffer Annual: Training* (Biech, 1972–2010). Two volumes are published each year, one for trainers and one for consultants. These resources and many others provide activities that you can easily adapt to the training program you are designing.

 (10 minutes)

3. **PPT** Show **slide 3-19**. Tell the participants that **handout 3-9** lists 10 categories of activities with a brief explanation of each, and a contest will determine which table group can identify the most specific activities. There are only two rules:

(1) You must have at least one activity in each category.

(2) You must be able to explain or demonstrate the activity if called upon.

Tell the participants that you will be walking around to clarify any of the categories if they wish. State that they have seven minutes to identify as many learning methods in all the categories they can and that a prize is involved. Yell "go" and begin to time them.

Examples of Activities

- *Presentations:* panels, tours, lecturettes, guided note taking, storytelling, and debates

- *Demonstrations:* instructor role plays, field trips, videos, DVDs, clips from movies, magic tricks, coaching, interviews, and props

- *Reading:* read-ahead materials, letters to each other, story starters, and Internet research

- *Dramatization:* skits, survival problem solving, costumes, and writing a script

- *Discussions:* buzz groups, round robins, brainstorming, nominal group technique, fishbowls, and develop a theory

- *Problem presentations and cases:* case studies, in baskets, critical incidents, sequential case studies, problem-solving clinics, and ELAs

- *Art:* portraits, cartoons, posters, draw a logo, and draw how you feel
- *Play-likes:* role plays, role reversals, video feedback, outdoor adventure, improvisations, and simulations
- *Games:* crossword puzzles, relays, card games, computer games, board games, and game-show adaptations
- *Participant-directed:* skill centers, teaching teams, self analysis, and research
- *Participative events:* icebreakers, energizers, and closers

4. At the end of seven minutes, call time. Ask each team to count its learning methods and then ask someone from the team with the most activities to read their activities to the group. The other teams can add some of these ideas to their own lists.

Award prizes and give everyone a round of applause. Ask the participants if they think they have enough ideas from which to choose.

(20 minutes)

I suggest that you give a prize to all of the teams.

Alternative. This activity doesn't need to be a competition; you could assign a couple of categories to each team to identify learning methods in each category.

Activity 3-8:   **Using KSAs for Instructional Design**

Selecting Activities Based on the KSA

📄 **Handout**   3-10, 3-11

✖ **Materials/Equipment**   None

🖳 **Slides**   3-20

🕐 **Time**   25 minutes

🗩 **Lead-In**   "How many of you are familiar with the abbreviation *KSA*?"

 Process

1.   Show **slide 3-20** and ask participants to turn to **handout 3-10**. Tell them that when they choose which learning method to use from the list they just developed, they should match the activity to the kind of learning that will occur: knowledge, skills, or attitude.

2. Present a brief lecturette about Benjamin Bloom and KSAs. Direct the participants' attention to the hierarchy of verbs at the bottom of the handout. Explain that this table presents the hierarchical order of the outcomes, using verbs to define the learning.

    Note: Each behavior becomes more complex as you move from left to right. Lead a discussion about how this corresponds with writing good learning objectives.

    Note: You may wish to mention that KSA originally stood for knowledge, skills, and attitudes. Somewhere along the line, someone changed the *A* to abilities, which has become accepted. As trainers, however, we should all know the origin of KSAs.

3. Ask participants to turn to **handout 3-11** and point out the tie-in between learning methods and KSAs. Say, "Form groups of three to five people based on the last digit of your telephone number. Take your handouts with you and find a comfortable place to sit. Decide which KSA addresses each activity best. For example, if you are trying to change an attitude, will a lecturette work best? It probably won't. If you are trying to impart knowledge, will a lecturette work for that? It probably will." Note that some of the learning methods will work well for more than one KSA.

    Note: You may want to have half of the room start at the top and work down, and the other half of the room start at the bottom and work up to save time.

     Process the activity after 10 minutes.

Possible Answers

The generally accepted answers are listed in this answer key.

LEARNING METHOD	KNOWLEDGE	SKILL	ATTITUDE
Lecturette	K		
Debate	K		A
Group discussion		S	A
Panel discussion	K		A
Brainstorming	K		
Case study	K	S	A
Role play		S	A
Demonstration	K		
Demonstration with practice	K	S	
Independent study	K		
Field trip	K		
Film and video	K		
Simulation		S	A
Game, exercise, or structured experience	K	S	A
Handouts and print materials	K		A
Hands-on practice		S	
Guided note taking	K		

4. As you wrap up this page of the handout, point out the camera graphic at the bottom. State again that the participants will find this "In Focus" graphic throughout their materials. Its purpose is to *focus* on the three things that participants must vary to maintain participants' interest: activities, participants in the groups, and size of the groups.

Activity 3-9: Developing Training Support Materials—Visuals

📄 **Handout** 3-12

✖ **Materials/Equipment** None

PPT **Slides** 3-21

🕐 **Time** 15 minutes

💬 **Lead-In** "Visuals help your participants grasp the point quickly, apply the concept to what they already know, and retain the information longer."

Process

1. 🎧 How many of you have seen props (like the magnifying glasses) used in training sessions? What is the most unusual item that you've used or seen others use? Consider a few examples.

2. State that although most of us rely on PowerPoint slides, we should remember to use other visuals such as props, DVDs, pictures, and so forth.

3. PPT 📄 Show **slide 3-21** and review briefly. **Handout 3-12** is meant as a resource and reminder. It provides tips to remember when you design your visuals, especially PowerPoint slides. Ask if they have any questions about designing visuals.

Activity 3-10:   Know Your Training Style

Training Style Self-Assessment

Training Style Self-Assessment Scoring

Pulling It All Together

Understand Your Training Style

Handout		3-13 through 3-17
Materials/Equipment		Flipchart
Slides		3-22 through 3-29
Time		45 minutes
Lead In		"How many of you know your training style?"

Process

1. Knowing your own training style preference helps you be a better trainer; it will also help you understand others' preferences so you can lead them into their comfort zones. Ask participants to turn to **handout 3-13**. Using **slide 3-22**, deliver a lecturette about the four dimensions of training: content, process, task, and people.

   (5 minutes)

2. Tell the participants to complete the self-assessment in **handout 3-14** using a 1–5 scale, with 1 meaning "not at all like me" and 5 meaning "most like me."

   (10 minutes)

3. Ask the participants to complete the scoring in **handout 3-15**. Discuss whether or not they agree with the results. They should complete the blanks in the middle of the page, for example:

   • The coaching style is concerned with content and people.

   • The guiding style is concerned with task and process.

- The facilitating style is concerned with process and people.

- The presenting style is concerned with content and task.

 (5 minutes)

Note: The "In Focus" at the bottom of the page identifies the four training styles: coaching, guiding, facilitating, and presenting.

4. **PPT** 📄 Use **slides 3-23** through **3-29** and **handout 3-16** to demonstrate that putting the two continuums together gives us the four training styles. Emphasize that all of the four styles are important for a successful training session. Although each of us has a preferred training style, we must be careful to take a balanced approach and also do those things we may not care to do.

5. 📄 Divide the participants according to their strongest training style and explain the relationships of the dimensions and the four styles. Ask participants to identify several advantages of their particular style and write it on the grid on **handout 3-16**. They should also identify the drawbacks of having a particular training style preference that is too strong. Allow 10 minutes and then ask each group to report and facilitate a discussion. List their responses on a grid on a flipchart to help the participants remember the content.

Note: The guiding style often has few or no participants. If this happens, you can ask for two or three participants who would like to take on the challenge.

Possible Responses

Here are some of the responses you can expect:

Coaching Strengths:

- supports the individual in the process

- motivates and encourages

- leads participants in the right direction

- has sincere enthusiasm and positive attitude

- easily encourages participation

- provides reinforcement naturally.

Coaching Cautions:

- may not bring closure to topics or sections

- may become the resource rather than the material that is taught

- may not be strong on content details

- may lack respect or credibility.

Guiding Strengths:

- states clear expectations and boundaries

- respects participants' active role in learning

- may be more appropriate for hard skills

- creates ground rules to hold difficult participants accountable

- gives systematic presentation and uses logical approach.

Guiding Cautions:

- may not be appropriate for soft skills

- may be less flexible during the presentation

- may not be aware of lagging interest or other dynamics

- has less ability to adapt when mechanicals malfunction.

Facilitating Strengths:

- encourages active participation

- has good listening skills

- tries to be on an equal level with participants

- encourages interaction

- embodies principles of Malcolm Knowles

- draws on and validates experiences.

Facilitating Cautions:

- may be less focused on content and too focused on discussion

- may have a short attention span

- may not be good with logistics

- may lose control

- may lose track of time.

Presenting Strengths:

- delivers interesting presentations

- enjoys being in front of a group

- is a positive influence

- is organized and in control

- is comfortable giving information

- engages group and thinks on his or her feet.

Presenting Cautions:

- may not enable or allow participants' self-discovery

- may have to deal with own ego

- may be manipulative or dominating

- may be too structured.

Note: These lists come directly from the 2005 *Training for Dummies*. Permission has been granted for them to be used in this Trainer's Guide.

(20 minutes)

6. Ask participants to turn to **handout 3-17** and complete it based on what they have learned about themselves and their training styles.

(10 minutes)

7. Transition statement, "Recognize that your training style will come face to face with a group of participants, all of whom have different learning styles. Think about your training style preference as we address learning styles in the next module."

Activity 3-11: Help! I've Been Asked to Conduct a Webinar! Focus on You—Wrap-Up of Module 3

Handout		3-18, 3-19
Materials/Equipment		None
Slides		3-30
Time		15 minutes
Lead-In		"We are wrapping up module 3."

Process

1. Ask participants to turn to **handout 3-18** and tell them that this is a resource for their future reading.

2. Show **slide 3-30** and have participants turn to **handout 3-19**. Ask them to take 15 minutes to capture their thoughts about this module.

3. When you see that most people have completed their notes, give a one-minute warning and ask them to turn to module 4.

PowerPoint Slides

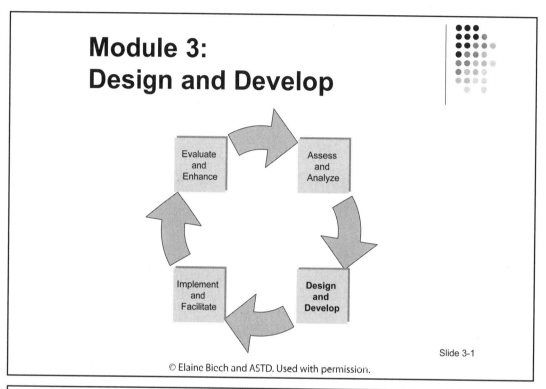

Module 3:
Design and Develop

Evaluate and Enhance

Assess and Analyze

Implement and Facilitate

Design and Develop

© Elaine Biech and ASTD. Used with permission.

Slide 3-1

Module 3 Objectives

- ## Apply adult learning principles to a training session.

Slide 3-2

Module 3 Objectives

- Apply adult learning principles to a training session.
- **Name at least a dozen learning methods.**

Slide 3-3

Module 3 Objectives

- Apply adult learning principles to a training session.
- Name at least a dozen learning methods.
- **Assess which learning method best meets the learners' needs.**

Slide 3-4

Module 3 Objectives

- **List the characteristics of effective PowerPoint slides.**

Slide 3-5

Module 3 Objectives

- List the characteristics of effective PowerPoint slides.

- **State the advantages and disadvantages of your training style.**

Slide 3-6

Adult Learning

I learned _____

because _____

Slide 3-7

Adult Learning Principles

1. Adults have a need to know why.

Slide 3-8

Adult Learning Principles

2. Adults enter with a self-concept.

Slide 3-9

Adult Learning Principles

3. Adults bring a wealth of experience.

Slide 3-10

Adult Learning Principles

4. Adults have a readiness to learn those things that help them cope.

Slide 3-11

Adult Learning Principles

5. Adults devote energy to those things that will help them.

Slide 3-12

Adult Learning Principles

6. Adults are responsive to internal motivators.

Slide 3-13

Adults:
Answer Their Questions

- Incorporate in the Design

- Incorporate in the Delivery

How?

Slide 3-14

Recommendations for Effective Training Design

- Objectives
- Limitations
- Content
- Sequencing the Content
- Establish Expectations Early
- Activities and Media

Slide 3-15

FOCUS Your Opening

- Facilitate Interest and Participation
- Offer Something About Yourself
- Clarify Expectations
- Understand Participant Needs
- State the Ground Rules

Slide 3-16

FOCUS Your Opening

- Facilitate Interest and Participation
- Offer Something About Yourself
- Clarify Expectations
- Understand Participant Needs
- State the Ground Rules

How can you accomplish these?

Slide 3-17

Focus on What's Happening!

- **Examine this train-the-trainer session through another lens:**
  - **What training techniques have you noticed?**
  - **What have you experienced?**
  - **What have you observed?**

Slide 3-18

Learning Method Categories

- How many learning methods can you name in each of these categories?

- List as many as you can.

Slide 3-19

Instructional Design: KSAs

- Knowledge

- Skill

- Attitude

Slide 3-20

Create Powerful PowerPoint Slides

- **Keep It Simple**
- **Use an Appropriate Font**
- **Select a Visual Theme**
- **Add Interest**
- **Check for Accuracy**

Slide 3-21

The Four Dimensions of Training

- Content

- Process

- Task

- People

Slide 3-22

Your Training Preferences

Content _____ Process

Slide 3-23

Your Training Preferences

Task

Content _____ Process

People

Slide 3-24

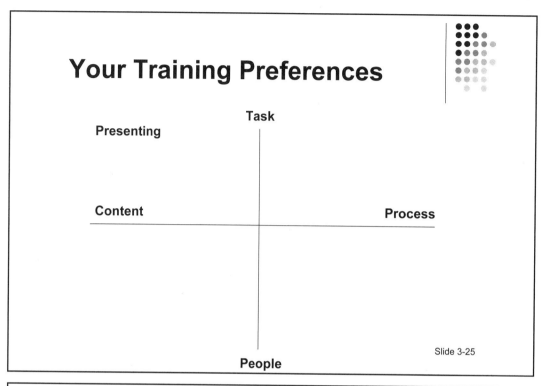

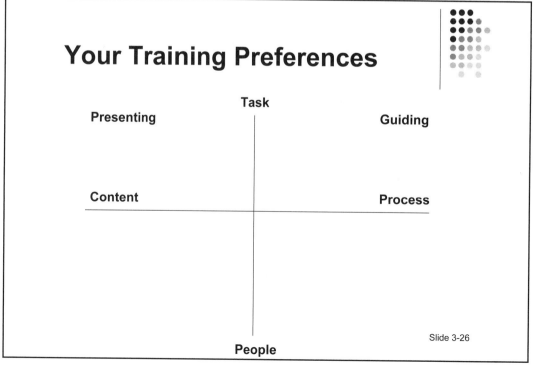

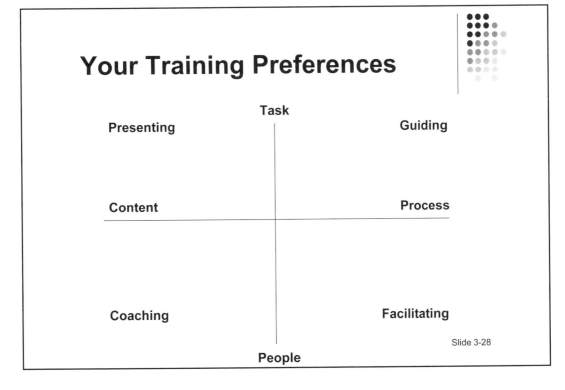

Four Training Styles

- Coaching Style

- Guiding Style

- Facilitating Style

- Presenting Style

Slide 3-29

Focus on You

What is important for your focus?

Slide 3-30

Trainer's Guide: Module 4— Implement and Facilitate

8

What's in This Chapter?

- Detailed step-by-step instructions to present the activities for Module 4—Implement and Facilitate

- Instructions to identify the equipment and material needs for each activities

- Instructions to determine the amount of time each activity requires

See chapter 5 for a general guide to facilitating a successful program.

Session at a Glance

Table 8-1. Module 4—Implement and Facilitate

Actual Time	Activity	Time	Participant Handout	Slide Number	Media/ Materials
	Activity 4-1: Introduction to Module 4—Implement and Facilitate How Do You Address Different Learning Styles in the Classroom?	30 min.	4-1, 4-2	4-1 through 4-10	
	Activity 4-2: How Do You Establish a Positive Learning Environment?	30 min.	4-3	4-11 through 4-16	
	Activity 4-3: Focus on What's Happening!	10 min.	4-4	4-17	
	Activity 4-4: Presenting a Dynamic Delivery	20 min.	4-5	4-18, 4-19	Flipchart
	Activity 4-5: What Are the Pros and Cons of Lectures?	25 min.	4-6		Flipchart
	Activity 4-6: Do You Get Nervous?	20 min.	4-7	4-20	
	Activity 4-7: Presentation Tools Demonstration	40 min.	4-8		Equipment as needed
	Activity 4-8: The Quandary Queue	55 min.	4-9	4-21	Flipchart
	Activity 4-9: Skill Practice Delivery Preparation	30 min.	4-10	4-22	Flipchart, other equipment as needed

continued on next page

Table 8-1. Module 4—Implement and Facilitate, *continued*

Actual Time	Activity	Time	Participant Handout	Slide Number	Media/ Materials
	End Day 2	.			
	Open Day 3	10 min.			
	Activity 4-10: Skill Practice Delivery Preparation Training/Facilitating Checklist	120–150 min.	4-10, 4-11	4-22	Flipcharts, other equipment as needed
	Activity 4-11: Questions, Questions, From All Perspectives	20 min.	4-12	4-23	
	Activity 4-12: How Do You Bring Closure to a Training Session?	20 min.	4-13	4-24	
	Activity 4-13: Focus on You—Wrap-Up of Module 4	15 min.	4-14	4-25	

Activity 4-1: Introduction to Module 4—Implement and Facilitate

How Do You Address Different Learning Styles in the Classroom?

Handouts 4-1, 4-2

Materials/Equipment None

Slides 4-1 through 4-10

Time 30 minutes

Lead-In "Let's turn to the Implement and Facilitate module."

Process

1. Ask participants to turn to **handout 4-1**. Use **slides 4-1** through **4-9** to provide an overview of the objectives for the module. Refer to any objectives that are related to the list of focus expectations that you posted on the wall during the opening activity.

2. After participants have looked at **handout 4-2**, show them **slide 4-10**. State that we all have different learning preferences and add some of the additional information found on the page, noting that David Kolb and Ned Herrmann have provided much of the research to support learning styles.

   Discuss with participants whether they can identify their learning styles; then ask them to complete and score the 15 questions. Check to see how many were surprised about their primary and secondary learning styles.

3. Ask participants to stand, take their books, put either their thumb or pinky in the air, and then find a partner at another table who is holding up the same finger. Tell them to buzz with their partner to identify one way that trainers could tap into each of the three learning styles. They should list them at the bottom of the page.

4. Ask the participants for examples.
   Here are some suggestions:

   - *Visual*: creating graphic models, drawing concepts, taking notes, viewing slides and flipcharts, watching movies, and using colorful paper or sticky notes

   - *Auditory*: spoken word, allowing them to talk, panel discussions, and music

   - *Kinesthetic*: things to manipulate such as modeling clay, crayons, Koosh balls, and paper that feels good.

Activity 4-2:	**How Do You Establish a Positive Learning Environment?**

Handout 4-3

Materials/Equipment None

Slides 4-11 through 4-16

Time 30 minutes

Lead-In "Creating a positive learning environment that is built on trust, respect, integrity, and success is claimed by many, but achieved by few. Why do you suppose that happens?"

 Process

1. Show **slide 4-11** and say, "What do trainers do that prevents the establishment of a positive learning environment?" Expect responses such as "putting content ahead of participants," "spoon-feeding everything, so that participants do not experience the learning first," or "failing to create a welcoming room." State that trainers can do five things and use **slides 4-12** through **4-16** to explain each one briefly.

2. Tell participants to choose a new partner. Assign each pair one of the categories on **handout 4-3**. Have them read the ideas about how to establish a positive learning environment.

3. Tell the partners to select the category that they believe is most important for establishing a positive learning environment. Say that we will use a technique called *funneling* to whittle down all the choices to just a few ways to establish a positive environment. Ensure that each pair has selected one that they believe to be the most important.

4. Have the partners stand and meet with another pair of partners. Each pair will explain why they believe their choice is the most important one. The four ultimately need to come to a conclusion and become one group of four.

5. The group of four meets with another group of four. The two groups present their selection, and the group of eight must come to a decision about which is the most important. If you have a group of 30 people or more, you may wish to conduct a round with another group of eight.

6. Stop the action, and ask the groups for their final decisions about the most important ways to establish a positive learning environment.

7. Sum up this activity by saying, "So, if you can't do it all, these are the two or three things you can do to establish a positive learning environment."

8. Have participants return to their seats and debrief the activity by asking what they see as the activity's purpose and when they might use funneling. Some possible answers are when

   • there are many final "best" answers

   • participants need to review concepts or hear others' ideas

   • participants need to move around.

9. Wrap up the activity by stating that the physical seating arrangement can either help or hinder establishing a positive learning environment. Ask participants to turn to the table on the next page of **handout 4-3**. Review the six seating arrangements and ask, "Can you think of a specific time when you might use each one during training sessions that you currently conduct?" Conduct a brief discussion to summarize, reminding them to consider both the physical and the psychological preparation of the environment.

Activity 4-3:   Focus on What's Happening!

📄 **Handout**   4-4

✖ **Materials/Equipment**   None

[PPT] **Slides**   4-17

⏰ **Time**   10 minutes

❞ **Lead-In**   "Time to stop and focus on what's happening in the session one last time."

🔢 **Process**

1. [PPT] 📄 Show **slide 4-17** and tell participants to turn to **handout 4-4**. State, "Once again, let's stop everything we are doing and *focus* on what we have experienced through another lens. We have just started the design phase, so think about this session through the designer's eyes. Use a magnifying glass and consider all the details that have gone into the design. Ask participants to write their ideas on **handout 4-4**. What have you noticed?"

2. As participants share their ideas, listen carefully. If explanations are required, give them. Answer questions where necessary. Share any errors you have made and tell participants how you intend to do it differently next time.

   Note: Take care not to become defensive.

3. You should expect to hear these things and others: They learned to divide participants into small groups in new ways, expect participants to take more risks, gather Day 1 evaluations and share information, ask for questions about the day before, stand at the door to say good-bye to each participant, select a team spokesperson, take time to answer questions, and all the other things you are doing right!

Remember!

You must select a few participants at lunch to play the disruptive roles during activity 4-8. Refer them to **handout 4-9**. More information is available to you on the handout.

Activity 4-4: Presenting a Dynamic Delivery

Handout 4-5

Materials/Equipment Four flipcharts posted on the walls with these titles:

- What They Hear: What's Good?
- What They Hear: What Needs to Change?
- What They See: What's Good?
- What They See: What Needs to Change?

Markers that will not bleed through paper (for example, Mr. Sketch)

Slides 4-18, 4-19

Time 20 minutes

Lead-In "How you present often becomes more important than what you present."

Process

1. Ask participants to turn to **handout 4-5**. Explain that dynamic delivery is made up of what we present, as well as how we present it. The quality of the presentation depends upon two things: what participants hear and what they see. Add an example for each.

2. Tell participants to count by fours in German, French, Spanish, Russian, or whatever language you know, to help them divide into four groups. (You may need to provide a quick lesson.) Assign each group one of the flipcharts. Ask them to identify several items that fit the category and then list them on the charts using markers that do not bleed through the paper.

3. After four minutes, call time and have the groups move clockwise around the room to the next chart. Repeat this two more times or until each group has had a turn at each chart. Ask for a finger vote to decide who will stay and report what is listed on their charts. (Finger vote: Team members put their right hands in the air with their index fingers pointing to the ceiling. On the count of five by the facilitator, team members lower their hands and point to the person who receives their vote; the person with the most fingers pointing at him or her wins the vote.) Other participants can be seated.

   Here are some examples, if you need to get participants started:

What They Hear: What's Good?

- volume heard easily throughout the room
- pitch (rolling like Colorado)
- varied pace—not too fast and not too slow
- pauses used appropriately, not afraid of appropriate silence, punctuates with pauses
- good articulation and pronunciation
- few or no fillers.

What They Hear: What Needs to Change?

- volume—too loud or too soft
- pitch (flat like Kansas)
- inappropriate pace—either too fast or too slow
- pauses—none used or at inappropriate times
- incorrect articulation or pronunciation
- fillers: um, ah, er, ya know.

What They See: What's Good?

- stance (planted firmly)
- appropriate movement—not repetitive, moves into the audience
- expressive gestures make a point
- animated or appropriate facial expression
- direct eye contact with all participants
- poise and confidence.

What They See: What Needs to Change?

- stance—swaying or crossing legs
- pacing or rocking movement
- gestures—stilted or distracting (for example, hands in pocket jingling change)
- deadpan or unusual facial expression
- fleeting or limited direct eye contact
- lack of poise (appears nervous).

4. 🔊 All of these details are critical because they send a message to the members of our audience, who interpret what they see and hear, and then make a judgment about the presenter. Ask the participants how they might view the presenter based on his or her delivery. Here are some adjectives to get the group started, if necessary:

- competent or incompetent

- strong or weak

- confident or unsure

- interesting or boring

- knowledgeable or unprepared

- relaxed or stressed

- sincere or insincere

- eloquent or inarticulate

- particular or indiscriminate

- interested or just earning a paycheck.

   State that the participants will make these judgments whether or not they are correct.

5. Wrap up the large group discussion by saying that although trainers are not professional speakers, we must all present information at some time or another. Therefore, we should determine ways to polish our presentation skills. One way to do that is to be professional about how we use notes.

6. 📄 State that the ideas for using notes at the bottom of **handout 4-5** are a resource for participants.

   PPT *Note:* **Slides 4-18** and **4-19** are for backup only.

Activity 4-5: What Are the Pros and Cons of Lectures?

Handout 4-6

Materials/Equipment Flipchart posted with debate timeline

Slides None

Time 25 minutes

Lead-In "As we discussed the way to polish presentation skills, the topic of lectures probably came to mind."

Process

1. Say, "You've probably noticed that we have been using the word *lecturette*. This modification suggests a shorter and more light-hearted version of the word *lecture*. Lectures or lecturettes can be either positive or negative."

2. Ask for two volunteers who will debate the merits of lecturettes. Ask the two debaters to select whether they want to debate the pros or the cons of lectures. Divide the room in half; each half should support one of the debaters. Explain that the participants, who form two support groups, are really the brains behind the debate. Each support group will provide content and arguments for its debater by creating a list of the pros or cons as appropriate. Tell the teams that you will give them five minutes to prepare.

   (10 minutes)

3. Place the debaters in the center or near the front of the room. Encourage the rest of the participants to take notes on **handout 4-6**. As the timekeeper, use the following guide, which includes breaks for the debaters to conference with their teams for ideas and support. Post this on a flipchart. You will track the times.

   Round One

   Cons 1.5 minutes opening

   Pros 1.5 minutes opening

   Cons 1 minute rebuttal

   Pros 1 minute rebuttal

   3 minute conference with teams

Round Two

Pros 1 minute commentary

Cons 1 minute commentary

Pros 0.5 minute response

Cons 0.5 minute response

3 minute conference with teams

Final Round

Pros 1.5 summary

Cons 1.5 summary

4. The debate is over after the time limit—a total of 17 minutes—is up. Ask for applause for each team. Declare that the debate was a tie!

5. Sum up by saying, "As you can see, there are pros and cons for providing a lecturette." Mention a couple of the points that each of the teams made in support of their argument.

Activity 4-6:   Do You Get Nervous?

📄 **Handout**   4-7

✖ **Materials/Equipment**   None

 Slides   4-20

⏰ **Time**   20 minutes

💬 **Lead-In**   "How many of you get nervous before training? Most of us do."

🔢 **Process**

1. Show **slide 4-20**. Tell the participants that several polls in the past have found that people are more afraid of speaking in front of groups than of dying, which suggests that people would rather die than train!

2. 📄 Note that **handout 4-7** provides a list of suggestions to address nervousness. Ask participants to take five minutes to peruse the page silently, highlighting or underlining anything that they find useful.

3. ⏰ After five minutes, ask participants what happens when they become nervous. Provide suggestions or ask the group for ideas to address any of the nervous symptoms.

4. Ask what was helpful to them on the handout they read.

5. Emphasize that participants will not want to eliminate the nervousness completely, because a little adrenalin will give them the winning edge.

Activity 4-7:   Presentation Tools Demonstration

Handout
4-8

Materials/Equipment
Presentation support materials and equipment

Slides
None

Time
40 minutes

Lead-In
"Most of us know how important visuals are to a presentation."

Process

1. As participants work in their table groups, ask them to select a visual support from the top of **handout 4-8** to demonstrate everything that could be done incorrectly. (Prevent duplicates if possible.)

2. Tell them to take 15 minutes to prepare a short presentation of all the things that could be done incorrectly using the visual support they have chosen.

   (15 minutes)

3. Each group should present its skit to the rest of the group. Follow each presentation with applause.

   (10 minutes)

4. Ask participants to turn to **handout 4-8**. Summarize this activity with a large group discussion that provides tips for using media and support materials. Encourage participants to list ideas.

   (10 minutes)

Activity 4-8: The Quandary Queue

Handout 4-9

Materials/Equipment Flipchart and markers

PPT Slides 4-21

Time 55 minutes

Lead-In "At times, the profession can be challenging."

Note: You should have chosen two disruptive participants earlier and given them directions that when you turn to **handout 4-9** you want them to begin their disruptive role. Ask one to be a negative know-it-all who disagrees with you. Ask the second one to be silent, refusing to respond to the group or to you. Be sure they understand that they need to keep the role a secret until you announce it.

Select the role players carefully:

- Choose no more than one per table to personalize the experience for each table.

- Assign a role that would be a reversal for the individual (for example, a quiet person may become aggressive, talkers may disengage).

- Select individuals who are "players."

Process

1. **PPT** Show **slide 4-21**. As participants turn to **handout 4-9**, ask what quandaries they find themselves in. List their challenges on the flipchart. Ask each group to select a situation and to identify suggestions to address it.

2. Facilitate their responses for the situations they selected. Add your examples and comments as appropriate.

 (25 minutes)

3. Ask about the kinds of difficult participants they encounter and list those on the flipchart. Ask for suggestions about how to handle each disruptive behavior.

Here are some suggested solutions:

- *Side conversations.* Walk behind them and present between them, direct a question to one of them.

- *Heckling.* Try to ignore, review ground rules, call a break and speak to the hecklers, hand them a marker and ask them to present.

- *Sniping/griping.* If negative, say, "Imagine what would have to happen to make it work?" several times; ask how others feel.

- *Argumentative.* Avoid escalation of disagreement, move on to another topic, declare a break.

- *Domineering.* Break eye contact, call on others, interrupt, acknowledge, and move to another person.

- *Clowning around.* Ignore as long as you can, present a serious question.

- *Uncooperative.* Pair with a fully cooperative person who is participating, ask for help from other participants, divide into smaller subgroups.

In all of these cases, a time may come when you need to pull the individual out of the session during a break to discuss. In some cases, you may be able to get to the root of the problem.

 (25 minutes)

4. Review the general guidelines for dealing with disruptive participants at the bottom of **handout 4-9**. Ask them to define the 3P goal in their own words:

- Problem elimination

- Preserving the climate

- Protecting self-esteem.

The critical thinking behind the 3P goal is that you must eliminate (or at least reduce) the problem. No matter what the strategy, trainers need to ensure that neither the person creating the problem, nor the rest of the participants, feel uncomfortable with how the situation is handled.

5. Model the best way to deal with the planted disruptive participants. At some point, another participant will state that something is unusual about the behaviors; if not, bring it up yourself. Discuss how the disruptive behavior of the plants was handled and what else might have been done.

6. If necessary, return to complete **handout 4-9**.

Note: The "In Focus" camera graphic presents the 3P goal of resolving problems. These are the three things you will want to do when faced with a problem participant:

- Eliminate the *Problem.*

- *Preserve* the climate.

- *Protect* the self-esteem of the participant.

7. You may wish to jokingly wrap up this activity by saying, "Of course, YOU never act up like this, but now you have suggestions for dealing with everyone else."

Activity 4-9:   Skill Practice Delivery Preparation

📄 **Handout**   4-10, 4-11

✖ **Materials/Equipment**   Resources for presentation content, such as articles or ASTD *Infolines* (see recommended *Infolines* listed below); whether you use articles or *Infolines*, the topics should relate to training
Index cards
Paper
Flipcharts
Markers
Other supplies for presenters
Flipcharts, one for each group that will work together

PPT **Slides**   4-22

⏰ **Time**   30 minutes

💬 **Lead-In**   "As was stated on the first day, tomorrow you will give a 10-minute presentation to your table group."

🔢 Process

1. PPT 📄 ✖   Display **slide 4-22** and tell participants that you have set aside 30 minutes for preparation. Review the instructions on **handout 4-10**. Here's what they should do:

   - Select one of the resources provided.

   - Prepare a 10-minute presentation based on one topic from the publication.

   - Select a topic that is new to them.

   - Plan a presentation with a beginning, a middle, and an end.

   - Write a learning objective.

   - Build in interaction and participation.

   - Plan to use at least one visual support (flipchart, handout, prop, or PowerPoint).

   - 📄 Note that the checklist on **handout 4-11** will be used to provide feedback from the rest of their group members (in activity 4-10)

- Decide what kind of feedback they would like to receive.

- Obtain materials, such as index cards or paper, from you.

2. Assign one flipchart to each group so that they can prepare pages on the same pad and will not need to remove them. Let them know that each group will present in a different room.

3. Tell the participants that they have time to prepare now and will have an additional 30 minutes to finalize their plans before their presentation. Ask for absolute silence during the preparation period; anyone who needs to speak with someone should leave the room.

    Here are some suggested ASTD *Infolines*. Each person in the small group should have a different resource:

- "Do's and Don'ts for the New Trainer," by Mary O'Neill

- "Accelerated Learning," by Deborah M. Fairbanks

- "Basics of Instructional Systems Development," by Chuck Hodell

- "Simulation and Role Play," by Marilyn Buckner

- "Basics of E-Learning," by Elisabeth Rossen and Darin Hartley

- "Effective Distance Learning," by Elizabeth C. Thach

- "Training and Learning Styles," by Susan Russell

- "Using Music as a Training Tool," by Lenn Millbower

- "Ethics for Trainers," by Jennie Johnson

- "Create Effective Job Aids," by Susan Russell

- "How to Create a Good Learning Environment," by Cat Sharpe

- "Effective Classroom Training Techniques," by Rick Sullivan and Jerry L. Wircenski

- "Make Every Presentation a Winner," by Jerry L. Wircenski and Richard L. Sullivan

- "How to Prepare and Use Effective Visual Aids," by Leanne Eline

- "How to Facilitate," by Don Aaron Carr

- "Transfer of Training," by Paul Garavaglia.

Activity 4-10:   Skill Practice Delivery Preparation

Training/Facilitating Checklist

🗋 **Handouts**   4-10, 4-11

✖ **Materials/Equipment**   Flipcharts, one for each table group that will work together
                                 Play-Doh on each table
                                 Other equipment as needed

PPT **Slides**   4-22

🕐 **Time**   150 minutes

❞ **Lead-In**   "Time has been set aside for your presentation."

🔢 **Process**

1. 🗋 PPT Review the instructions on **handout 4-10** with the participants, displaying **slide 4-22**.

   - Present in your table teams.

   - Prepare and make a 10-minute presentation.

   - Content must be from a provided resource.

   - Plan to use visual support.

   - Facilitator has supplies.

2. 🕐 State the schedule and post it on a flipchart:

   - Total of 120–150 minutes

   - First 30 minutes for final prep

   - 10 minutes for each presentation

   - 🗋 5–7 minutes for feedback to each person, using the Training/Facilitating Checklist in **handout 4-11**.

   - Each small group will build in their own 15-minute break.

3. Point out that Play-Doh has been added to each table as a new tactile item, as well as an energy and nervousness releaser.

4. Maintain silence during the 30 minutes of prep time. During this time, you may need to coordinate the use of flipcharts, projectors, and so forth. At the end of the 30 minutes, assign rooms or space for each group. Remind presenters to ask before their presentation if they seek specific feedback. Assign a specific time to return to the large group.

(35 minutes)

5. During the small group presentations, walk from group to group to ensure that they stay on schedule and to determine whether you can assist in any way. Be careful not to walk in during someone's presentation.

(100 minutes)

Note: You need to allow time the previous day to provide the resources and explain the process.

Activity 4-11: Questions, Questions, From All Perspectives

📄 **Handout**   4-12

✖ **Materials/Equipment**   None

 Slides   4-23

🕐 **Time**   20 minutes

❞ **Lead-In**   "Asking questions, answering questions, and encouraging participants to ask questions: All are skills that you will use."

🔢 **Process**

1. 📄 **PPT** Ask the participant to turn to **handout 4-12**. Get an overview of the material, show **slide 4-23**, and tell the participants to read through the information on the page. Ask what questions they have about the material.

2. If you have time, have participants identify a couple of appropriate questions to add to a topic they teach. They could pair up and share their questions to get feedback from another participant.

Activity 4-12:	**How Do You Bring Closure to a Training Session?**

 Handout   4-13

Materials/Equipment   None

PPT **Slides**   4-24

Time   20 minutes

Lead-In   "What's important when you bring closure to your session?"

Process

1. **PPT** Show **slide 4-24** and obtain several comments from participants about what should be accomplished when you end a training session.

2. Share two or three creative ways you have closed sessions. Be sure to tell participants why you used those particular activities at that particular time.

3. Have participants turn to **handout 4-13** to review the ideas found there. Ask them to write down some a few of their own ideas for implementing the closing steps. Allow 3–5 minutes, then ask for additional ideas.

4. Wrap up by suggesting that a good closure technique is to gather everyone's email address to distribute after the session. This allows networking and learning to continue.

Activity 4-13:   Focus on You—Wrap-Up of Module 4

📄 **Handout**   4-14

✖ **Materials/Equipment**   None

PPT **Slides**   4-25

🕐 **Time**   15 minutes

💬 **Lead-In**   "We are wrapping up module 4."

🔢 **Process**

1. PPT 📄 Show **slide 4-25** and tell the participants to take 15 minutes to capture their thoughts about this module on **handout 4-14**.

2. 🕐 When you see that most people have completed their notes, give a one-minute warning and ask them to turn to module 5.

PowerPoint Slides

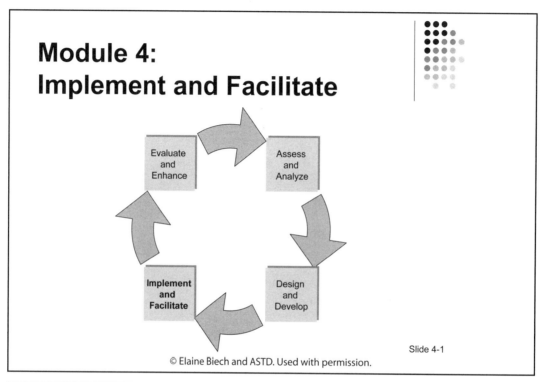

Module 4:
Implement and Facilitate

Slide 4-1

© Elaine Biech and ASTD. Used with permission.

Module 4 Objectives

- **Discuss different learning styles.**

Slide 4-2

Module 4 Objectives

- Discuss different learning styles.
- **Establish a positive learning environment.**

Slide 4-3

Module 4 Objectives

- Discuss different learning styles.
- Establish a positive learning environment.
- **Evaluate effective presentation skills.**

Slide 4-4

Module 4 Objectives

- Discuss different learning styles.
- Establish a positive learning environment.
- Evaluate effective presentation skills.
- **List advantages and disadvantages of lecturettes.**

Slide 4-5

Module 4 Objectives

- **Use visuals appropriately.**

Slide 4-6

Module 4 Objectives

- Use visuals appropriately.
- **Recall techniques to manage nervousness.**

Slide 4-7

Module 4 Objectives

- Use visuals appropriately.
- Recall techniques to manage nervousness.
- **Resolve problem classroom situations.**

Slide 4-8

Module 4 Objectives

- Use visuals appropriately.
- Recall techniques to manage nervousness.
- Resolve problem classroom situations.
- **Ask and answer questions that lead to learning.**

Slide 4-9

Learning Styles

- **Visual**

- **Auditory**

- **Kinesthetic**

How can you address each of these?

Slide 4-10

Establish a Positive Learning Environment

Slide 4-11

Establish a Positive Learning Environment

• Create a Safe Haven for Learning

Slide 4-12

**Establish a Positive
Learning Environment**

**• Create a Comfortable
Environment**

Slide 4-13

**Establish a Positive
Learning Environment**

• Encourage Participation

Slide 4-14

Establish a Positive Learning Environment

- **Facilitate More Than You Present**

Slide 4-15

Establish a Positive Learning Environment

- **Encourage Participants to Track Their Own Progress**

Slide 4-16

Focus on What's Happening!

- Examine this train-the-trainer session through another lens:
  - What training techniques have you noticed?
  - What have you experienced?
  - What have you observed?

Slide 4-17

Presenting a Dynamic Delivery

- **What They Hear**
  - Volume
  - Pitch
  - Pace
  - Pauses
  - Articulation
  - Fillers

Slide 4-18

Presenting a Dynamic Delivery

- **What They See**
  - **Stance**
  - **Movement**
  - **Gestures**
  - **Facial Expression**
  - **Eye Contact**
  - **Poise**

Slide 4-19

Do You Get Nervous?

What works for you?

Slide 4-20

Quandary Queue

What challenges do you encounter?

Slide 4-21

Skill Practice Information

- Total of 120–150 minutes
- First 30 minutes for final prep
- 10 minutes for each presentation
- 5–7 minutes for feedback to each person
- Each small group will build in their own 15-minute break

Slide 4-22

Asking and Answering Questions

Slide 4-23

Bring Closure

- **What do you want to accomplish?**

Slide 4-24

Trainer's Guide: Module 5— Evaluate and Enhance

9

What's in This Chapter?

- Detailed step-by-step instructions for presenting the activities for Module 5—Evaluate and Enhance

- Instructions to identify the equipment and materials needed for each activity

- Instructions to determine the amount of time each activity requires

See chapter 5 for a general guide to facilitating a successful program.

Session at a Glance

Table 9-1. Module 5—Evaluate and Enhance

Actual Time	Activity	Time	Participant Handout	Slide Number	Media/Materials
	Activity 5-1: Introduction to Module 5— Evaluate and Enhance	5 min.	5-1	5-1 through 5-4	
	Activity 5-2: The Importance of Evaluation Evaluating Progress Kirkpatrick's Four Levels of Evaluation	35 min.	5-2 to 5-4	5-5 through 5-7	
	Activity 5-3: Why Return-on-Investment?	15 min.	5-5	5-8	
	Activity 5-4: Evaluate and Enhance	20 min.	5-6		
	Activity 5-5: Focus on You—Wrap-Up of Module 5 Congratulations to Me!	70 min.	5-7, 5-8	5-9, 5-10	Envelopes, evaluations, certificates

Activity 5-1: Introduction to Module 5—Evaluate and Enhance

Handout 5-1

Materials/Equipment None

Slides 5-1 through 5-4

Time 5 minutes

Lead-In "Let's turn to the Evaluate and Enhance module."

Process

1. Ask participants to turn to **handout 5-1**. Use **slides 5-1** through **5-4** to provide an overview of the objectives for the module.

2. Refer to any objectives that are related to the list of focus expectations that you posted on the wall during the opening activity.

Activity 5-2: The Importance of Evaluation

Evaluating Progress

Kirkpatrick's Four Levels of Evaluation

📄 **Handout**	5-2 through 5-4
✖ **Materials/Equipment**	None
PPT **Slides**	5-5 through 5-7
🕐 **Time**	35 minutes
💬 **Lead-In**	"We are starting the final module, Evaluate and Enhance. This module asks whether we accomplished what we set out to accomplish."

🔢 Process

1. 📄 PPT Ask participants to turn to **handout 5-2**, show **slide 5-5**, and provide a brief overview of evaluation and why it is important.

2. 📄 PPT Next, ask participants to turn to **handout 5-3**. Show **slide 5-6** and list all the things that could be measured in this train-the-trainer program in the left column.

   🕐 (10 minutes)

3. 💬 Ask participants to share their ideas with someone with whom they have not yet worked. After they share, select an idea from each list and identify how they could measure it. Have the pair decide who has spoken the least; that will be the person who reports for the pair. Ask for several examples.

   🕐 (10 minutes)

4. 📄 PPT Introduce Kirkpatrick's four levels of training in **handout 5-4**, using **slide 5-7**. Ask the participants to identify how each could be measured. Here are some suggestions:

   • Level 1: Questionnaire and webinar

   • Level 2: Self-assessment, facilitator assessment, simulation, case study, and exercises

   • Level 3: Interview, focus group, on-site observations, and follow-up questionnaire

   • Level 4: Tools that measure business performance (sales, expenses, and rework) with the ability to isolate the impact of training.

   🕐 (10 minutes)

Activity 5-3: Why Return-on-Investment?

📄 **Handout**   5-5

✖ **Materials/Equipment**   None

 Slides   5-8

⏰ **Time**   15 minutes

❞ **Lead-In**   "What is ROI?"

🔢 **Process**

1.   📄 Display **slide 5-8**. Respond to several of the comments and ask participants to turn to **handout 5-5**.

2. Review the five steps that outline the ROI process. Create a short discussion with questions such as these:

    - What is the benefit of measuring ROI?

    - Where do the data come from?

    - What is the key to ROI?

    - What is the benefit to the organization?

    - What are the benefits to you as a trainer?

    - Do you have any other thoughts about ROI?

3. Wrap up by recommending one of the books written by Jack Phillips, such as *Show Me the Money* (2007) or *Beyond Learning Objectives: Develop Measurable Objectives That Link to the Bottom Line* (2008).

Activity 5-4:   Evaluate and Enhance

 Handout   5-6

Materials/Equipment   None

PPT Slides   None

Time   20 minutes

Lead-In   "Let's remember the *enhance* aspect of this module."

Process

1. Ask participants to turn to **handout 5-6** and ask, "What do you believe the *enhance* aspect of this module means?"

2. Review the ideas on the handout.

3. Ask, "What ideas do you have that will continue to enhance your professional development?" Facilitate a discussion, using ideas from the participants. You may wish to add a few of these ideas:

   • Identify ways to leverage your skills and knowledge to create opportunities in the future.

   • Become technologically savvy.

   • Invest in acquiring skills and knowledge that you might be able to use in the long term.

   • Stay focused on the big picture.

   • Be clear about both your personal needs and your professional needs.

4. Summarize by noting the "In Focus" at the bottom of the page and ask participants if they know the 3Cs of a great trainer. State that a great trainer is credible, competent, and confident. End the discussion by saying, "Let's take some time now to *focus* on you."

Activity 5-5: Focus on You—Wrap-Up of Module 5

Congratulations to Me!

Handouts 5-7, 5-8

Materials/Equipment
No. 10 envelope for each participant
Evaluation for each participant
Certificate for each participant

Slides 5-9, 5-10

Time 70 minutes

Lead-In "We are wrapping up the session."

Process

1. Go to the Expectation flipchart page that is hanging on the wall. Ask if you have fulfilled all of their expectations (of course, you have completed each of them or have a plan to do so). Respond to any concerns or questions.

   (10 minutes)

2. Show **slide 5-9** and tell the participants to take 20 minutes to capture their thoughts about this module on **handout 5-7** and to create a personal action plan.

   (20 minutes)

3. When you see that most people have completed their action plans, give a one-minute warning and ask them to find someone with whom they would like to work one last time. Ask the participants to work in pairs or trios to share their action plans and to obtain additional ideas for strategies. Tell them they will have 15 minutes.

   (15 minutes)

4. Ask the participants to return to their places; then show **slide 5-10** and ask them to turn to **handout 5-8**. State, "We often leave a learning situation with good intentions to change our behavior, but when we return to the workplace, we have to answer 15 voice messages and 100 emails. So, we reluctantly put the training manual on the shelf and forget about our good intentions."

   Continue with, "We have a plan to remind you of your good intentions. **Handout 5-8** gives directions to design a congratulations card for you. Take 10 minutes to fill in the blanks; identify at least two things you'd like to accomplish within the two-month time period. Use the crayons and the markers to decorate your card."

5.   While participants are decorating their cards, hand an envelope to each person.

6. Once participants have completed their cards, ask them to self-address the envelopes and place the cards inside. Tell them that you will mail the cards back in six to eight weeks to remind them of what they wanted to do. Collect the cards for future mailing. As the last few participants complete their cards, ask for volunteers to share the things they will focus on once they return to work.

   (15 minutes)

7. Pass out the evaluations; ask participants to complete them and leave them at the door on their way out.

8. Before they leave, ask the participants to form a circle in the middle of the room (or in a hallway if there isn't enough room). Pass out the certificates at random and ask each person to check to be sure that the certificate does not have his or her name on it. Start with one person and ask him or her to present the certificate to the person whose name is on it, offer congratulations, and give the individual a personal "wish of focus" related perhaps to something that happened during the training. For example, one participant might say, "Congratulations, Dan, I hope that you will be able to focus on getting that job you've told us about," or "Congratulations, Rhea, you are a great listener and I hope that you will be able to focus on building more confidence." You may also suggest a future predictions focus, as in "Mason, I predict that in five years you will be focusing on your boss's job!"

9. Once all the certificates have been distributed, wish the participants well and stand at the door to say good-bye to everyone.

PowerPoint Slides

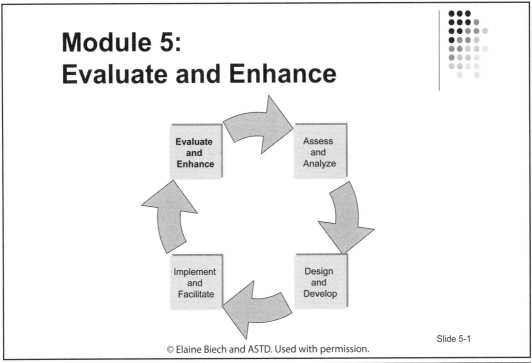

Module 5:
Evaluate and Enhance

Evaluate and Enhance

Assess and Analyze

Design and Develop

Implement and Facilitate

© Elaine Biech and ASTD. Used with permission.

Slide 5-1

Module 5 Objectives

- **Explain Kirkpatrick's four levels of evaluation.**

Slide 5-2

Module 5 Objectives

- Explain Kirkpatrick's four levels of evaluation.

- **Discuss the ROI for training efforts.**

Slide 5-3

Module 5 Objectives

- Explain Kirkpatrick's four levels of evaluation.

- Discuss the ROI for training efforts.

- **Establish a personal development plan for your continuous learning.**

Slide 5-4

The Importance of Evaluation

Slide 5-5

Evaluating Progress

What Could You Measure?

Slide 5-6

Kirkpatrick's Four Levels of Evaluation

- Level 1: Participant Reaction
- Level 2: Test to Verify Learning Objectives Were Achieved
- Level 3: Application and Transfer of Learning
- Level 4: Business Impact

Slide 5-7

Return-on-Investment

Slide 5-8

Focus on You

What is important for your focus?

Slide 5-9

Congratulations to Me!

- Two things you'd like to accomplish within two months.

- Decorate your congratulations card.

Slide 5-10

Alternative-Length Delivery Modules 10

What's in This Chapter?

- 19 single-topic presentations that range from 30 minutes to two hours
- Select topic-based modules to meet required learning objectives
- Two full-day sessions for basic train-the-trainer content
- 10 opening and five closing ideas

▲　　▲　　▲

Do you have a specific objective in mind? Perhaps you have a group of trainers who need to practice writing learning objectives, or maybe your department is going to be involved in the design process. This chapter identifies 19 topic-based subjects that you can use as stand-alone training sessions or combine with each other to design your own training day.

The participant handouts in chapter 11 and on the CD can be used for a variety of training needs and timeframes. This chapter will present a number of scenarios and suggest the handout(s) you might use. The situations vary from 90 minutes to half-day sessions.

These training sessions are designed for a specific purpose. You will need to go to chapter 11 to locate the handout number, which is easy because they are all in numeric order.

Chapters 5–9 contain the portions of the Trainer's Guide that provide the instructions for what to do. You just need to read the directions and prepare for your session. Of course, the PowerPoint slide numbers will be listed on the Trainer's Guide activity.

Even though the sessions are shorter, it's still important to conduct a brief opening and closing activity. If your group has 10 to 12 people and they know each other from past training experiences, plan on about 15 minutes to open and 15 minutes to close. You can use one of the ideas listed here or create your own.

10 Quick Opening Ideas

Depending upon your group, you may want to start with a quick opening that addresses what they have already learned in some of the train-the-trainer modules. You could ask each person to address one of these questions:

1. What is one thing you need to learn about our topic today?

2. Share with us your greatest hope for today.

3. Our topic today is _____. What is one tip you could share with all of us?

If the group needs to get to know each other better, you could open with one of these fill- in-the-blank icebreakers, or you can make up some of your own:

4. My dream vacation would be _____.

5. The last book I read was _____, and I thought it was _____.

6. On Saturdays, my favorite activity is to _____.

7. I feel best when people _____.

8. If I had to choose a second career, I would like to _____.

9. If I could be invisible for one day, I would _____.

10. If I could have any view from my home, it would be _____.

Five Ways to Close With Pizzazz

Think about what you want to accomplish with your closing. Do you want to set goals, plan to stay in touch, make a commitment to action, share positive feedback, or just say good-bye? Here are a few ideas:

1. If you want participants to set goals, give each person a postcard. Have them self-address the postcards and write a goal or two on it. Collect the postcards and say you will mail them back to them in a month to remind them of their goals.

2. If you want them to stay in touch, get everyone's email address and create an email list. Tell the participants that you will send the first email; it will have a tool attachment that will help them with the content you covered during the session.

3. If you want them to make a commitment, have participants write a memo to their bosses about what they learned and what they want to do in the future.

4. If you want them to share positive feedback, give everyone several gold stars and have them move around to other members of the group, stick a gold star on their handouts, and tell them how they earned the gold star.

5. If the closing is to say good-bye, have them stand in a circle and share their best moment of the session with the rest of the group.

Short Topic-Based Sessions

There may be times when you need to conduct training on only one topic. Perhaps you are a training department supervisor or coach who needs a single hard-hitting topic to enhance participants' skills or knowledge in one topic area. Perhaps trainers have recently been assigned added responsibilities, or some employees need to enhance their skills in a particular area. If you are working with a subject matter expect (SME) who will conduct training, some of these topics may be helpful. The topics are designed to be used by supervisors during a staff meeting or even as conference presentations by ASTD Chapters.

Listed in tables 10-1, 10-2, 10-3, 10-4, and 10-5 are several objectives and accompanying activities. The amount of time required is listed, as well as the handouts and slides you would use. Remember that you will also need to add time for an opening and a closing activity.

Considerations

- Topics are listed in order of how they are presented in the participant material.

- Although the slide number is listed, you can easily use a flipchart instead.

- Additional time has been added to the original activities to allow for more discussion.

Table 10-1. Short Topic-Based Session: Module 1—Introduction

Objective	Activity	Time	Participant Handout	Slide Number
To introduce the ADDIE concept	Activity 1-2: What Does a Trainer Do?	60 min.	1-3, 1-4	1-8
To introduce temporary trainers to training	Activity 1-3: What Is Training?	45 min	1-5	1-9, 1-10

Table 10-2. Short Topic-Based Session: Module 2—Assess and Analyze

Objective	Activity	Time	Participant Handout	Slide Number
To introduce needs assessment To teach to basics of data collection	Activity 2-2: Needs Assessment and Analysis Basics	60 min.	2-2 to 2-5	2-6 through 2-16
To assist seasoned trainers with creating a needs assessment	Activity 2-3: How Can You Collect Data? What Questions Will You Ask? Is Training the Solution?			
To provide an instrument to self-assess training skills	Activity 2-4: Participant's Personal Needs Assessment	50 min.	2-6	2-17, 2-18
To write SMART learning objectives	Activity 2-6: What Constitutes a Good Learning Objective? How Do You Write a Learning Objective? What Are Your Personal Objectives?	50 min.	2-8 to 2-10	2-20 through 2-28

Table 10-3. Short Topic-Based Session: Module 3—Design and Develop

Objective	Activity	Time	Participant Handout	Slide Number
To introduce design to new designers To introduce the idea of applying adult learning principles to designing training	Activity 3-2: Introducing Design and Adult Learning Principles Malcolm Knowles and Adult Learning Principles Adult Learning—Answer Their Questions Activity 3-3: Six Recommendations for Effective Training Design	90 min.	3-2 to 3-5	3-7 through 3-15

continued on next page

Table 10-3. Short Topic-Based Session: Module 3—Design and Develop, *continued*

OBJECTIVE	ACTIVITY	TIME	PARTICIPANT HANDOUT	SLIDE NUMBER
To discuss what constitutes a good opening	Activity 3-4: FOCUS Your Openings for Added Value What's an Icebreaker?	50 min.	3-6, 3-7	3-16, 3-17
To introduce a variety of activities	Activity 3-7: Activities—Countless Alternatives to Lecture	60 min.	3-9	3-19
To introduce KSAs and their importance to design	Activity 3-8: Using KSAs for Instructional Design Selecting Activities Based on the KSA	40 min.	3-10, 3-11	3-20
To discuss formatting easy-to-read PowerPoint slides	Activity 3-9: Developing Training Support Materials—Visuals	30 min.	3-12	3-21
To help participants identify their training style— its positives and negatives	Activity 3-10: Know Your Training Style	60 min.	3-13 to 3-17	3-22 through 3-29

Table 10-4. Short Topic-Based Session: Module 4—Implement and Facilitate

OBJECTIVE	ACTIVITY	TIME	PARTICIPANT HANDOUT	SLIDE NUMBER
To discuss how learning styles affect training delivery	Activity 4-1: How Do You Address Different Learning Styles in the Classroom?	45 min.	4-2	4-10
To identify ways to create a learning environment that is conducive to learning	Activity 4-2: How Do You Establish a Positive Learning Environment?	50 min.	4-3	4-11 through 4-16
To discuss presentation skills	Activity 4-4: Presenting a Dynamic Delivery	40 min.	4-5	4-18, 4-19

continued on next page

Table 10-4. Short Topic-Based Session: Module 4—Implement and Facilitate,
continued

Objective	Activity	Time	Participant Handout	Slide Number
To discuss the appropriate use of a lecture	Activity 4-5: What Are the Pros and Cons of Lectures?	50 min.	4-6	
To help trainers overcome nervousness	Activity 4-6: Do You Get Nervous?	30 min.	4-7	4-20
To create an opportunity to discuss problems in the training room	Activity 4-8: The Quandary Queue	70 min.	4-9	4-21
To introduce new trainers to stand-up skills of training	Activity 4-10: Skill Practice Delivery Preparation Training/Facilitating Checklist	120 minutes plus prep	4-10, 4-11	4-22
To encourage trainers to ask more questions To help trainers feel comfortable with Q&A sessions	Activity 4-11: Questions, Questions From All Perspectives	30 min.	4-12	4-23

Table 10-5. Short Topic-Based Session: Module 5—Evaluate and Enhance

Objective	Activity	Time	Participant Handout	Slide Number
To introduce the basics of evaluation	Activity 5-2: The Importance of Evaluation Evaluating Progress Kirkpatrick's Four Levels of Evaluation Activity 5-3: Why Return on Investment?	70 min.	5-2 to 5-5	5-5 through 5-8

One-Day Training Sessions

At times, you may need a longer training session; then you can select from the activities above (tables 10-1 through 10-5) to create your own training for trainers. At other times, you may need to present only the basics. Tables 10-6 and 10-7, in this section, cover two of the most used training topics:

- "Presenting Training" (table 10-6) can be used to introduce new trainers to stand-up training.
- "Content Design" (table 10-7) can be used to introduce trainers or others to the concepts of training design.

Remember that you still have to select an opening activity and a closing activity for your session. Each allows for three 10–15 minute breaks. You may need to adjust the times slightly based on your group and the length of your day.

Table 10-6. One-Day Training Session: Presenting Training

Objective	Activity	Time	Participant Handout	Slide Number
To discuss how learning styles affect training delivery	Activity 4-1: How Do You Address Different Learning Styles in the Classroom?	30 min.	4-2	4-10
To identify ways to create a learning environment that is conducive to learning	Activity 4-2: How Do You Establish a Positive Learning Environment?	30 min.	4-3	4-11 through 4-16
To discuss presentation skills	Activity 4-4: Presenting a Dynamic Delivery	30 min.	4-5	4-18, 4-19
To discuss the appropriate use of a lecture	Activity 4-5: What Are the Pros and Cons of Lectures?	50 min.	4-6	
To help trainers overcome nervousness	Activity 4-6: Do You Get Nervous?	30 min.	4-7	4-20
To create an opportunity to discuss problems in the training room	Activity 4-8: The Quandary Queue	55 min.	4-9	4-21
To practice stand-up skills of training	Activity 4-10: Skill Practice Delivery Preparation Training/Facilitating Checklist	120 min.	4-10, 4-11	4-22
To help trainers feel comfortable with Q&A sessions	Activity 4-11: Questions, Questions, From All Perspectives	20 min.	4-12	4-23

Table 10-7. One-Day Training Session: Content Design

Objective	Activity	Time	Participant Handout	Slide Number
To introduce the ADDIE concept	Activity 1-2: What Does a Trainer Do?	40 min.	1-3, 1-4	1-8, 1-9
	Activity 1-3: What Is Training?		1-5	1-10
To introduce needs assessment	Activity 2-2: Needs Assessment and Analysis Basics	40 min.	2-2	2-6, 2-7
To teach to basics of data collection	Activity 2-3: How Can You Collect Data? What Questions Will You Ask? Is Training the Solution?		2-3 through 2-5	2-8 through 2-16
To provide an instrument to self-assess training skills	Activity 2-4: Participant's Personal Needs Assessment	50 min.	2-6	2-17, 2-18
To write SMART learning objectives	Activity 2-6: What Constitutes a Good Learning Objective? How Do You Write a Learning Objective? What Are Your Personal Learning Objectives?	30 min.	2-8 to 2-10	2-20 through 2-28
To introduce the idea of applying adult learning principles to designing training	Activity 3-2: Introducing Design and Adult Learning Principles Malcolm Knowles and Adult Learning Principles Adult Learning—Answer Their Questions	75 min.	3-2 through 3-4	3-7 through 3-14
	Activity 3-3: Six Recommendations for Effective Training Design		3-5	3-15
To discuss what constitutes a good opening	Activity 3-4: FOCUS Your Openings for Added Value What's an Icebreaker?	30 min.	3-6, 3-7	3-16 through 3-17
To introduce a variety of activities	Activity 3-7: Activities—Countless Alternatives to Lecture	40 min.	3-9	3-19
To introduce KSAs and their importance to design	Activity 3-8: Using KSAs for Instructional Design Selecting Activities Based on the KSA	25 min.	3-10, 3-11	3-20
To discuss formatting easy to read PowerPoint slides	Activity 3-9: Developing Training Support Materials—Visuals	20 min.	3-12	3-21

Participant Materials for a Complete Three-Day Session

11

What's in This Chapter?

- Introduction to the participant content
- Thumbnails of participant handouts for quick reference (full-size handouts are included on the CD)

▲　　▲　　▲

Introduction to the Participant Content

The three-day train-the-trainer session is divided into five modules:

1. Introduction
2. Assess and Analyze
3. Design and Develop
4. Implement and Facilitate
5. Evaluate and Enhance

All of the participant handouts required to conduct the five modules are in this chapter—whether you conduct the complete three-day session or shorter sessions. The easiest part for you is that the numbers and titles match the Trainer's Guide in chapters 5 through 9. Each participant handout has a number and a title at the top of the first page (most handouts are only one page in length, but a few are longer). The double number refers to the number of the module and the number of the handout within the module. For example, handout 3-13 is the thirteenth handout in module 3—Design and Develop.

In addition, the title at the top of the participant handout matches the activity name in the Trainer's Guide (chapters 5 through 9). So, if you see "What's an Icebreaker?" at the top of the participant hand-out, you will see the same title at the top of the Trainer's Guide activity.

This chapter contains thumbnails of all participant handouts for the train-the-trainer workshop. All of the handouts are available in full size on the CD. If you conduct a workshop that lasts a day or longer, we recommend that you print and copy the handouts you require (from the CD) and place them in a three-ring notebook for your participants.

You may customize some of the handouts with your own content. You may not, however, use any copyright symbol other than the ASTD copyright symbol already on the page.

It is wise to read all these handouts, answer the questions, and work through some of the activities before you conduct the train-the-trainer workshop. This will give you some idea of what you might want to brush up on first.

The complete set of participant handouts is listed here and on the CD.

Handouts for Train-the-Trainer Activities

Module 1: Introduction

Handout 1-1: Where's the Training Focus?
Handout 1-2: Agenda Review
Handout 1-3: What Does a Trainer Do?
Handout 1-4: What Is Training?
Handout 1-5: The Train-the-Trainer Workshop Modules
Handout 1-6: Focus on You—Wrap-Up of Module 1

Module 2: Assess and Analyze

Handout 2-1: Introduction to Module 2—Assess and Analyze
Handout 2-2: Needs Assessment and Analysis Basics
Handout 2-3: How Can You Collect Data?
Handout 2-4: What Questions Will You Ask?
Handout 2-5: Is Training the Solution?
Handout 2-6: Participant's Personal Needs Assessment
Handout 2-7: Focus on What's Happening!
Handout 2-8: What Constitutes a Good Learning Objective?
Handout 2-9: How Do You Write a Learning Objective?
Handout 2-10: What Are Your Personal Learning Objectives?
Handout 2-11: Focus on You—Wrap-Up of Module 2

Module 3: Design and Develop

Handout 3-1: Introduction to Module 3—Design and Develop
Handout 3-2: Introducing Design and Adult Learning Principles
Handout 3-3: Malcolm Knowles and Adult Learning Principles
Handout 3-4: Adult Learning—Answer Their Questions
Handout 3-5: Six Recommendations for Effective Training Design
Handout 3-6: FOCUS Your Openings for Added Value

Handout 3-7: What's an Icebreaker?

Handout 3-8: Focus on What's Happening!

Handout 3-9: Activities—Countless Alternatives to Lecture

Handout 3-10: Using KSAs for Instructional Design

Handout 3-11: Selecting Activities Based on the KSA

Handout 3-12: Developing Training Support Materials—Visuals

Handout 3-13: Know Your Training Style

Handout 3-14: Training Style Self-Assessment

Handout 3-15: Training Style Self-Assessment Scoring

Handout 3-16: Pulling It All Together

Handout 3-17: Understand Your Training Style

Handout 3-18: Help! I've Been Asked to Conduct a Webinar!

Handout 3-19: Focus on You—Wrap-Up of Module 3

Module 4: Implement and Facilitate

Handout 4-1: Introduction to Module 4—Implement and Facilitate

Handout 4-2: How Do You Address Different Learning Styles in the Classroom?

Handout 4-3: How Do You Establish a Positive Learning Environment?

Handout 4-4: Focus on What's Happening!

Handout 4-5: Presenting a Dynamic Delivery

Handout 4-6: What Are the Pros and Cons of Lectures?

Handout 4-7: Do You Get Nervous?

Handout 4-8: Presentation Tools Demonstration

Handout 4-9: The Quandary Queue

Handout 4-10: Skill Practice Delivery Preparation

Handout 4-11: Training/Facilitating Checklist

Handout 4-12: Questions, Questions, From All Perspectives

Handout 4-13: How Do You Bring Closure to a Training Session?

Handout 4-14: Focus on You—Wrap-Up of Module 4

Module 5: Evaluate and Enhance

Handout 5-1: Introduction to Module 5—Evaluate and Enhance

Handout 5-2: The Importance of Evaluation

Handout 5-3: Evaluating Progress

Handout 5-4: Kirkpatrick's Four Levels of Evaluation

Handout 5-5: Why Return-on-Investment?

Handout 5-6: Evaluate and Enhance

Handout 5-7: Focus on You—Wrap-Up of Module 5

Handout 5-8: Congratulations to Me!

Handout 1-1. Where's the Training Focus?

Training must focus on myriad things: the trainer, participant, content, and organization. Which area do you want to focus on, and what, specifically, do you need to learn in this session?

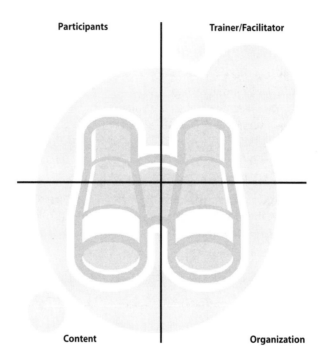

Handout 1-2. Agenda Review

Day 1   **Introduction**
   Welcome
   What's a Trainer?

   Assess and Analyze
   Needs Assessment Basics
   Participant's Personal Needs Assessment
   Writing Learning Objectives

   Design and Develop
   Adult Learning Theory
   Instructional Design
Day 2   Focus Your Opening
   Training Styles

   Implement and Facilitate
   Establishing a Positive Learning Environment
   Presentation Skills and Facilitation Techniques
Day 3   Skill Practice Delivery
   Managing Difficult Situations and Participants
   Asking and Answering Questions

   Evaluate and Enhance
   Evaluating Progress
   Enhancing the Experience and the Learning
   Continuous Learning: Where Do You Go From Here?

Train-the-Trainer Objectives

The purpose of the train-the-trainer workshop is to ensure that you will be able to
- list the characteristics of an exceptional trainer
- discuss the phases of a training cycle
- conduct a training needs assessment
- write correct learning objectives
- explain what is meant by adult learning theory
- design a participant-centered training experience
- implement a variety of learning activities
- establish a positive learning environment
- demonstrate the appropriate use of visuals
- evaluate effective presentation skills
- name Kirkpatrick's four levels of evaluation
- develop an individualized development plan for yourself.

Handout 1-3. What Does a Trainer Do?

Training is one of the most exciting jobs in the world. Here are some of the characteristics of a trainer:
- is both intuitive and rational
- understands both the business and the people of the organization
- is confident as well as empathetic
- can stick to schedules but can also improvise when necessary
- has a long-term focus and an immediate-need awareness
- can focus on a group but does not lose sight of the individuals
- is realistic, as well as creative.

A trainer is a process expert who is self-sufficient, flexible, organized, inclusive, and efficient. A trainer can be described as having many other characteristics, as well.

A trainer has excellent communication skills: the ability to present information, motivate employees, give feedback, create a learning climate, analyze needs, design learning opportunities, and evaluate results.

A trainer may also play a variety of roles, such as instructional designer, media designer, organization and development specialist, performance analyst, executive coach, courseware designer, performance improvement technologist, technical trainer, consultant, and, of course, corporate trainer.

Training can be one of the most exciting jobs; it can also be one of the most frustrating jobs.

Think back to your experiences as a trainer. Identify the frustrations and the pleasures of being a trainer and list several here:

Pleasures of a Trainer

Frustrations of a Trainer

© Elaine Biech and ASTD. Used with permission.

Handout 1-4. What Is Training?

Training is based on a model called instructional systems design (ISD). The original ISD model dates back to World War II, when the U.S. military required a model to develop quick and effective training for the use of sophisticated equipment. Although the original model has been improved upon slightly, the basic premise is so fundamental and logical that it's hard to argue for change. The five phases in the model are analysis, design, development, implementation, and evaluation (ADDIE).

ANALYSIS

This phase comprises needs assessment and analysis, which are used to identify the business goals and performance gaps that must be addressed. They also identify information about the participants, the work environment, and constraints that might affect the training effort, such as the budget. Once you assess the needs of the learners, you can develop the learning objectives.

DESIGN

The learning objectives in the analysis phase tell you what content should be covered; the design activities help you determine how to present the content. The objectives will identify the kinds of activities that will best accomplish the objectives. Although this workshop assumes that training is the best solution, you may find that training is not actually required. Instead, another solution, such as coaching, might be used. The root cause of the problem may be motivation or a lack of resources. In this phase, you decide how to structure the content, which method or blended methods you will use, and how to present the content.

DEVELOPMENT

The key activity in this phase is to convert the plans from the design phase into the materials required to implement the class, such as a participant book; handouts; a facilitator's guide; support materials, such as role plays or case studies; and media support, for example, PowerPoint slides. Although this workshop focuses primarily on a classroom setting, you may also be preparing for an e-learning situation. In addition, a subject matter expert (SME) may review the materials or hold a pilot course to work out the kinks in the program.

IMPLEMENTATION

This is the phase that initially comes to mind when many people answer the question, "What is training?" The implementation is more than just standing in front of the group and delivering content. The trainer must establish a positive learning climate, facilitate questions and activities, exude enthusiasm and confidence, and ensure that both the group needs and individual needs are met. During this phase, you will need to market the session, review the materials, practice the activities, perhaps learn new content, maintain the course to ensure that it continues to serve its purpose, schedule rooms, set up the training room, schedule equipment, print materials, schedule webinar time, and perform other supporting activities that ensure the delivery and implementation run smoothly.

EVALUATION

The last phase is critical to ensure that the training session meets the goals that were originally established. Using Donald Kirkpatrick's model, you will assess the training based on four levels: reaction, learning, transfer, and business results. Your organization may also use a return-on-investment (ROI) evaluation process. In addition, you should conduct a self-evaluation of your performance. The knowledge you gain in the fourth phase is used to confirm or redefine your purpose in the first phase.

These five ADDIE phases essentially become our process for the rest of this train-the-trainer workshop. Except for combining the design and development phases into one, we will dedicate a module to each phase in ADDIE. The diagram in handout 1-5 depicts the four key modules of this training:

- Assess and Analyze
- Design and Develop
- Implement and Facilitate
- Evaluate and Enhance.

Handout 1-5. The Train-the-Trainer Workshop Modules

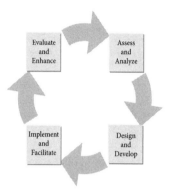

Think about your job as a trainer. What percentage of your time do you spend in each of the four areas?

Assess and Analyze ....

Design and Develop ....

Implement and Facilitate ....

Evaluate and Enhance ....

Handout 1-6. Focus on You—Wrap-Up of Module 1

1. What is the most important thing you have learned in this module?

....

....

....

....

....

2. What will you implement or change as a result of what you have learned?

....

....

....

....

....

3. What resources will you require to do what you would like?

....

....

....

....

....

4. Who could help you?

....

....

....

....

....

5. What questions do you have that need answers?

....

....

....

....

....

Handout 2-1. Introduction to Module 2—Assess and Analyze

ASSESS AND ANALYZE MODULE OBJECTIVES

By the end of this module, you will be able to
- explain the fundamentals of conducting a needs analysis
- identify questions used in a needs assessment
- assess your personal development needs
- develop correct learning objectives.

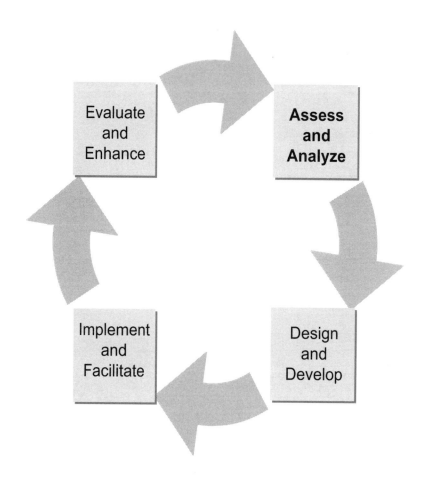

Handout 2-2. Needs Assessment and Analysis Basics

Don't let the terms *needs assessment* or *analysis* scare you. You conduct needs assessments and analyze the data every day. Are you missing an ingredient for vegetable soup? You will need to make a decision about whether to go to the grocery store to purchase the item, substitute another ingredient and hope no one notices, cook something else, or go out to dinner. Are you thinking about reseeding your lawn? You will need to learn about the cost and kind of seeds, what time of year is best, whether to do it yourself or hire someone, what equipment you will need, or whether to consider sod instead. In both cases, you conduct a needs assessment and analyze the data you have gathered.

Going on a vacation? Adopting a pet? Planning a party? Returning to college? Buying new appliances? Refinancing your house? Changing jobs? Taking tennis lessons? Each requires assessment and analysis, and you will complete five steps before you make a decision. Let's use taking a trip to a foreign country as an example:

1. Identify a need or problem. (You want to take a trip to a foreign country.)
2. Determine a plan for gathering data. (Determine who you will contact, what information you will need, and how soon you have to decide.)
3. Gather the data. (Talk to people who have traveled to this country, contact a travel agent, research the country on the computer, and keep notes about the information you learn.)
4. Analyze the data you collected. (How safe is the trip? Can you afford the trip? What time of year is best?)
5. Make a decision. (Decide whether or not to go on the trip. If yes, use the data you gathered to plan your trip.)

WHY CONDUCT A NEEDS ASSESSMENT?

As you did to prepare for your trip, a trainer needs to gather data to make wise decisions. Here are the steps trainers need to take:

- Clearly define the problem.
- Determine whether training can solve the problem.
- Identify the performance that is desired.
- Determine the root cause of the problem.
- Establish a baseline.
- Identify the scope of the training.

WHY ELSE MIGHT YOU CONDUCT A NEEDS ASSESSMENT?

....

....

....

....

....

....

....

Handout 2-3. How Can You Collect Data?

You may use many tools to conduct a needs assessment. What are the advantages or disadvantages of each?

Data Collection Method	Description	Advantages	Disadvantages
Interview	Discussions with people who understand the need		
Focus Group	Key people interviewed in a group		
Questionnaire	Electronic or paper-and-pencil survey questions		
Observation	Visually observing the employees or the situation		
Performance Data Review	Examination of previously collected statistics such as employment records		
Informal Discussion	Conversations that are more casual than an interview		
Knowledge Test	Exams that assess skills or abilities		

Note: You may use a combination of the tools listed.

Handout 2-4. What Questions Will You Ask?

Like a reporter, you need to analyze the why, who, what, where, when, and how of training. You might ask thousands of questions. As a trainer, you must identify what is most important and what you need to know so that you can recommend a learning event that is most beneficial to the participants, as well as to the organization. One of the most important reasons for conducting a needs assessment and analyzing the data is to determine whether training is the answer. If it is, the focus will be on the learner—your participant.

Here's an initial needs assessment that is a good start to most potential training situations. Why might each of these questions be helpful?

Two and a Half Dozen Questions to Consider

How will the responses to the following questions help you make decisions about the requested training?

Why

- Describe the problem.
- Why do you believe this is a problem? Describe the symptoms that you notice.
- What do you believe is causing the problem?
- Why do you believe this is a training problem?
- What performance gap needs to be addressed?
- How does the performance affect the organization?
- What organizational aspects might affect this situation?
- How does this training address business goals?
- How will you know when you have been successful?

Who

- What can you tell me about the audience (for example: age, education, and time with the organization)?
- What role and responsibilities do the participants have in the organization?
- What can you tell me about their work environment?
- Have the employees done this correctly in the past?
- Which instruments, materials, and equipment do the employees use?
- How do these employees feel about their performance?
- Who are the experts in the group?
- Could the training have disadvantages for the participants?

What

- Have you considered any off-the-shelf training?
- Have the employees had training on this or a related topic?
- What's the worst thing that will happen if we do not provide training?
- What other solutions have you considered?
- What other organizations (or departments) are experiencing this problem?

continued on next page

Handout 2-4. What Questions Will You Ask?, *continued*

WHERE

- Where will the training be conducted?
- Where will the subject matter expert be during the training?
- What special equipment will be necessary at the training session?

WHEN

- What is your timeline, and how long do you anticipate the course to continue?
- What are the timing issues (for example: length, start date, frequency, and vacation)?

HOW

- What resources are available for this training?
- Who is the decision maker for this training?
- How will the employees' skills and knowledge be supported following the training?
- How supportive are the participants' direct supervisors? How supportive is other management?

In Focus: Six Needs Assessment Questions

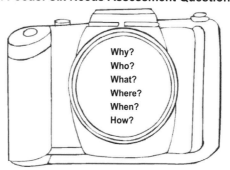

Why?
Who?
What?
Where?
When?
How?

Handout 2-5. Is Training the Solution?

The analysis is complete once you know whether it can be considered to be a "training need." These three quick questions will help you pinpoint the answer:

1. Does the individual have the skill to do the job?
2. Does the individual have the will to do the job?
3. Is the individual allowed to do the job?

If the answer to the first question is "no," training may be a solution, but not necessarily. If the answer to all of the questions is "yes," it is definitely not a training solution.

What else could it be?

- A "no" to the second question means you may have a motivation problem; training will not solve that.
- A "no" to the third question means there is probably a procedure or policy problem; training will not solve that.
- A "yes" to all three questions could mean that it is an equipment problem that prevents individuals from producing at the required level.
- Even a "no" to the first question does not necessarily mean training is required; perhaps coaching is a solution, or the individual has not received feedback.

Don't assume that a request for training really requires training; there might be dozens of other causes: language barriers; miscommunication; inadequate materials, tools, or workspace; unreliable equipment; unclear expectations; inappropriate consequences or incentives; lack of feedback or coaching; inappropriate job assignment; or others.

Important

Before you complete your needs assessment, be sure to determine whether training is the solution. Just because someone has requested training does not mean that training is required.

Handout 2-6. Participant's Personal Needs Assessment

Here's what this training skills and knowledge inventory is designed to help you do:
- identify the skills you require to perform your job effectively
- determine your current strengths and weaknesses
- assist you in setting specific objectives for your professional development.

INSTRUCTIONS

1. **Evaluate your ability** by completing column 1, using the rating scale below:
   5 — outstanding ability (one of my outstanding talents)
   4 — above-average ability (compared with my ability in other areas)
   3 — average or moderate ability
   2 — minimal ability
   1 — no experience or training in this area.
2. **Describe the importance of this skill to your training** by completing column 2:
   5 — one of the most important skills when I train
   4 — above-average importance
   3 — average importance
   2 — occasional importance
   1 — minimal importance
   0 — no importance.

Assessing Training and Development Needs

SKILL	YOUR ABILITY	IMPORTANCE ON THE JOB	DIFFERENCE
Design a needs assessment plan			
State which needs assessment method to use			
Conduct a task analysis to determine training needs			
Diagnose training and development needs to set program priorities			
Determine whether to buy training or develop in-house			
When purchasing programs from vendors, determine which program to select			
Assess performance before and after training to measure training results			
Link business needs to training outcomes			
Scores			

continued on next page

Handout 2-6. Participant's Personal Needs Assessment, *continued*

Design and Develop Training

SKILL	YOUR ABILITY	IMPORTANCE ON THE JOB	DIFFERENCE
Establish learning objectives			
Design or customize programs to satisfy specific needs			
Design effective visual support			
Apply adult learning theory and instructional principles in developing programs			
Evaluate and create participative instructional methods, such as role plays and demonstrations			
Design techniques to ensure transfer of learning to the job			
Describe own training style and state its impact on different learning styles			
Design effective openings and closings			
Scores			

Implement and Facilitate Training

SKILL	YOUR ABILITY	IMPORTANCE ON THE JOB	DIFFERENCE
Use effective presentation skills			
State appropriate time and best techniques when lecture is required			
Use group facilitation techniques			
Manage difficult participants			
Ask and answer questions			
Use visuals appropriately			
Manage unexpected classroom events			
Establish a positive learning environment			
Scores			

continued on next page

Handout 2-6. Participant's Personal Needs Assessment, *continued*

Evaluate and Enhance Training

SKILL	YOUR ABILITY	IMPORTANCE ON THE JOB	DIFFERENCE
Evaluate learning procedures and outcomes			
Name Kirkpatrick's four levels of evaluation and explain how to implement each one			
Use feedback to enhance future training			
Develop evaluation instruments, such as questionnaires and tests			
Analyze evaluation results			
Discuss the basic principles of ROI			
Scores			

MAINTAINING MY EDGE

Talents

Review your ratings in column 1. Put a plus next to those items for which you rated yourself 5.

List below four talents you can build on:

1. _____
2. _____
3. _____
4. _____

Development Needs

Subtract column 2 from column 1. Put the answer in column 3. Include the minus sign if it is a negative number. For example, if you rated yourself 2, and the importance 4, the total in column 3 is -2. The larger the negative number, the greater the need for improvement.

List below the four development needs you most want to work on:

1. _____
2. _____
3. _____
4. _____

The maximum score in column 1 is 150. An overall score of 120 or more in column 1 indicates a proficient instructor, although any rating of 3 or less indicates an area in which skills need to be improved.

Handout 2-7. Focus on What's Happening!

It's time to stop what you are doing and focus on what we have been doing through another lens. You have been observing this session through a participant's eyes. Now think about how you would examine this session through the designer's eyes. Use a magnifying glass and consider all the details that have gone into the design. Think about what has been happening in the room from the designer's perspective. What have you noticed?

- What training techniques have been modeled?
- What trainer/facilitator skills have been used?
- What design aspects have been incorporated?
- How has the trainer established a room conducive to learning?
- What's working?
- What's not working?
- What would you be doing right now if you were the trainer?

Handout 2-8. What Constitutes a Good Learning Objective?

Use the information gathered in the needs assessment to write learning objectives. Learning objectives are written to specify the desired performance (knowledge or skill) of the learner once training has been completed.

An objective should meet several criteria:
- *Specific*: It should be specific so that there is no question about what you mean, and it should use words that can be observed or heard.
- *Measurable*: It should be measurable, which means you can either count it or determine that it was or was not completed.
- *Attainable*: An objective should be attainable. It should not be too difficult, yet it should not be too easy.
- *Relevant*: It should be relevant to the organization and to the change that is desired.
- *Timely*: A good objective is time bound; that is, it should have a limit that states when the participant is expected to achieve the objective.

The first letter of each of these spells SMART. Objectives should be SMART.

Specific

Measurable

Attainable, yet a stretch

Relevant

Time-bound

Handout 2-9. How Do You Write a Learning Objective?

An objective can easily be written by filling in the blanks in this easy-to-remember question:

Who will *do what,* by *when,* and *how well*?

"*You* will *be able to write learning objectives* by *the end of this module 100 percent of the time.*"

Here's a formula that some trainers use called the ABCDs of a good objective:
- *Audience* (who)
- *Behavior* (will do what)
- *Condition* (by when or some other condition, such as with assistance)
- *Degree* (how well).

As you can see, the two methods require identical information.

Examine these objectives and determine which include all the components of a correct objective:

1. Participants will understand how to write learning objectives.

   ....
   ....
   ....
   ....

2. Participants will be able to name Kirkpatrick's four levels of evaluation 100 percent of the time.

   ....
   ....
   ....
   ....

3. You will be able to develop a training needs assessment upon request, using this participant manual as a guide.

   ....
   ....
   ....
   ....

4. At the end of this session, participants will be able to demonstrate techniques to deal with classroom problems 80 percent of the time.

   ....
   ....
   ....
   ....

Handout 2-10. What Are Your Personal Learning Objectives?

Use the results from your self-assessment to write at least three learning objectives for yourself. Use the formula:

Who will *do what,* by *when,* and *how well.*

LEARNING OBJECTIVE 1

....

....

....

LEARNING OBJECTIVE 2

....

....

....

LEARNING OBJECTIVE 3

....

....

....

Are Your Objectives SMART?
Specific?
Measurable?
Attainable, yet a stretch?
Relevant?
Time bound?

Evaluate your learning objectives. Does each meet the SMART criteria for a good objective?

CRITERIA	OBJECTIVE 1	OBJECTIVE 2	OBJECTIVE 3
Specific			
Measurable			
Attainable			
Relevant			
Time Bound			

Handout 2-11. Focus on You—Wrap-Up of Module 2

1. What is the most important thing you have learned in this module?

   ....
   ....
   ....
   ....
   ....

2. What will you implement or change as a result of what you have learned?

   ....
   ....
   ....
   ....
   ....

3. What resources will you require to do what you would like?

   ....
   ....
   ....
   ....
   ....

4. Who could help you?

   ....
   ....
   ....
   ....
   ....

5. What questions do you have that need answers?

   ....
   ....
   ....
   ....
   ....

Handout 3-1. Introduction to Module 3—Design and Develop

> **DESIGN AND DEVELOP MODULE OBJECTIVES**
>
> By the end of this module, you will be able to
> - apply adult learning principles to a training session
> - name at least a dozen learning methods
> - assess which learning method best meets learners' needs and learning objectives
> - list the characteristics of effective PowerPoint slides
> - state the advantages and disadvantages of your individual training style.

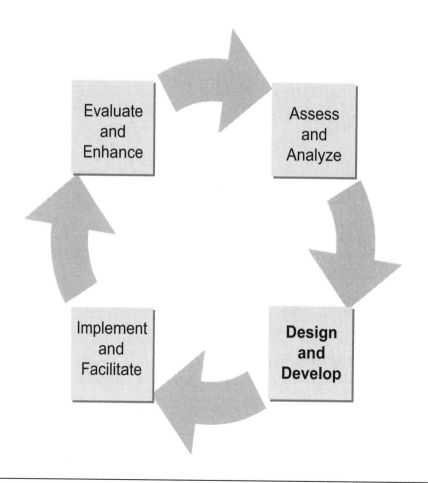

Handout 3-2. Introducing Design and Adult Learning Principles

Designing training programs is critical to the success of the program. A designer needs to have these characteristics:
- Be either an expert in the content or have the skills to draw the information out of a subject matter expert (SME).
- Have a big-picture perspective, as well as an eye for the details.
- Be both logical and creative.
- Apply adult learning principles as well as comprehend the role of a trainer.

As you can see, it takes a well-rounded person to be a successful training designer. Let's begin by exploring what it means to understand adult learning principles.

UNDERSTAND ADULT LEARNING PRINCIPLES

Identify three things you learned in the past two months and why you learned them. List them here:

1. I learned ....

   because ....

2. I learned ....

   because ....

3. I learned ....

   because ....

What did you discover about the way you learn?

....

....

....

....

....

....

In Focus: Good Design ABCs

**Get Their Attention
Practice Behavior
Give Them
Confidence**

Handout 3-3. Malcolm Knowles and Adult Learning Principles

Malcolm Knowles is considered the father of adult learning theory in the United States. He took the topic of adult learning from theory to practice with his adult learning theory assumptions. Knowles popularized the word *andragogy* to describe the growing body of knowledge about how adults learn. First published in 1973 (and now in its third edition), his easy-to-read book, *The Adult Learner: A Neglected Species* (1984), took the topic from theoretical to practical.

Here are some things that Knowles believed about adults:

- Adults have a *need to know* why they should learn something before they invest time in a learning event. As trainers, we must ensure that learners know the purpose for training as early as possible. Participants need to know how this information and content will affect them and why they should care.
- Adults enter any learning situation with a *self-concept* of themselves as self-directing, responsible grown-ups. As trainers, we must help adults identify their needs and direct their own learning experience.
- Adults come to a learning opportunity with a wealth of *experience* and a great deal to contribute. Trainers will be more successful if they identify ways to build on and make use of adults' hard-earned experience.
- Adults have a strong *readiness to learn* those things that will help them cope with daily life effectively. Training that relates directly to situations adults face will be viewed as more relevant.
- Adults are willing to devote energy to learning those things that they believe will *help them* perform a task or solve a problem. Trainers who determine needs and interests, and then develop content in response to these needs, will be most helpful to adult learners.
- Adults are more responsive to internal *motivators*, such as increased self-esteem, than to external motivators, such as higher salaries. Trainers can ensure that this internal motivation is not blocked by barriers such as a poor self-concept or time constraints by creating a safe learning climate.

These assumptions lead to the kinds of questions participants ask themselves when entering a training session:

- Why do I need to know this?
- Will I be able to make some decisions, or are you going to recreate my grade-school memories?
- Why am I here? Why is she here? What do they think they can teach me?
- How is this going to simplify my life? How will this make my job easier?
- Do I want to learn this? How will it help me?
- Why would I want to learn this? Am I open to this information?

Handout 3-4. Adult Learning—Answer Their Questions

As trainers, we must address the questions our learners have—not in words, but in the actions that occur as the result of a good training design or training delivery. What can you do as you design or deliver training that will address these questions and deal with your participants' concerns?

QUESTIONS	INCORPORATE IN DESIGN	INCORPORATE IN DELIVERY
1. Why do I need to know this?		
2. Will I be able to make some decisions, or are you going to re-create my grade-school memories?		
3. Why am I here? Why is she here? What do they think they can teach me?		
4. How is this going to simplify my life? How will this make my job easier?		
5. Do I want to learn this? How will it help me?		
6. Why would I want to learn this? Am I open to this information?		

Handout 3-5. Six Recommendations for Effective Training Design

Getting started with the design can be easier if you think about these suggestions:

1. **Objectives:** Base the training on your learning objectives.
2. **Limitations:** Remember the constraints that limit the design, including time, money, and support.
3. **Content:** Use the resources available to you for content: SMEs, books, your own experience, or off-the-shelf materials. Use a mind map to create a list of potential topics.
4. **Sequencing the Content:** Select a topic sequence that will enable the learner to acquire the content: easy to hard, job order, less risky to more risky, chronological, problem-solution, broad to specific, priority order, build on a concept, or others.
5. **Establish Expectations Early:** Ensure that the first 30 minutes of your design sets the stage for the rest of the design. If you expect participation, get participation early. If it will be fast-paced, begin with a fast pace.
6. **Activities and Media:** The key is to take advantage of the hundreds of activities, such as case studies, games, role plays, demonstrations, puzzles, and discussions, and incorporate as many as you can. How do you select them? Consider the audience (who, how many, and what they know); the objectives (skill, knowledge, and attitude); your style; the time of day; time available; the location; dependability; and the sequencing of other activities.

DESIGN CHECK

Use the report card to grade this train-the-trainer workshop. Provide examples for why you rated it the way you did.

GOOD DESIGN ELEMENT	GRADE	EXAMPLES
Based on objectives		
Solid, accurate content		
Sequencing is logical		
Opening clarified purpose		
Participant interaction was clarified early		
Variety of activities were used		
Pace of activities varies		
Participants contribute to activities		
Practical; can be transferred to the workplace		
Visuals support the learning		
Content addresses what I need or want to learn		
Comments		

continued on next page

Handout 3-5. Six Recommendations for Effective Training Design, *continued*

A template, like this one, provides a "Module at a Glance" to organize your design.

Module_____	Design the Opening _____		Time _____	125 minutes_____	
OBJECTIVES:					
• Identify how to apply adult learning principles to a training session.					
• List critical elements in the opening session.					
• Review content.					

TOPIC/CONTENT	LEARNING METHOD	MATERIALS/MEDIA	TIME	PAGES
Applying Adult Learning Principles	Individual Activity; Small Group Discussion	PowerPoint	30 minutes	14
Opening Critical Elements	Role Play and Discussion	Role-Play Cards	60 minutes	15–17
Break			15 minutes	
Content Review	Relay Race	2 flipcharts, prizes	20 minutes	NA

What features of this template would make it useful for design and then later for delivery?

Handout 3-6. FOCUS Your Openings for Added Value

Design the opening of your training session so that it uses the time wisely. It should add focus to the event, accomplishing these five things:

FACILITATE INTEREST AND PARTICIPATION

- Help everyone get to know each other.
- Establish a participative climate.
- Set the stage so participants will know what to expect, for example, fun, serious, fast, or participative.
- Encourage networking with introductions that communicate something about each participant.

OFFER SOMETHING ABOUT YOURSELF

- Establish your credibility.
- Communicate your experience.
- Participate with everyone else by providing an example.
- Let participants know something about you personally.

CLARIFY EXPECTATIONS

- Present the agenda.
- Introduce the objectives for the session.
- Consider an activity that asks participants about their expectations for the session and post them.
- If you will be unable to meet all expectations, tell your participants and offer an alternative.

UNDERSTAND PARTICIPANT NEEDS

- Conduct a mini needs assessment to learn more about participants' experience, expertise, or knowledge.
- Refer to information that you gathered prior to the session, for example, "Several of you stated that you would like to learn…."
- Ask questions of groups and individuals.

STATE THE GROUND RULES

- Wait to hold the ground rules discussion until after you have created some interaction, but don't wait too long.
- Save time by stating your given ground rules; participants can add others.
- Ground rules written on a flipchart can be posted for all to see and for you to refer to if necessary.

It is worth your time to perfect the design (and delivery) of the opening. You want to "wow" your participants right from the start. If you focus your opening, it should have these characteristics:

- It should be practical, yet creative.
- It should be informative, as well as exciting.

How can you accomplish these five goals in your opening?

....

....

....

....

....

Handout 3-7. What's an Icebreaker?

An icebreaker is a short activity that occurs at the beginning of a session. An icebreaker gives participants an opportunity to interact with each other, to learn something about each other, and ideally to explore the topic. It is called an icebreaker because its key purpose is to help participants warm up.

People may think that the purpose is merely fun, and many icebreakers are fun. As a trainer, however, you want to add value to your opening by selecting an icebreaker that does these things:

ESTABLISHES THE CLIMATE
- encourages individuals to participate immediately
- sets the tone and climate for your session.

SUPPORTS YOUR PARTICIPANTS
- creates a nonthreatening way for participants to meet each other
- lets participants know what to expect.

IS CONGRUENT WITH THE CONTENT
- sets a compatible mood for the content
- introduces and generates interest about the content
- answers questions about the content
- creates curiosity about the content.

FACILITATES YOUR ROLE
- introduces your role as a facilitator
- helps you determine the characteristics of your participants
- decreases your nervousness as you begin the session.

You will find that some of your participants don't like icebreakers. They may even groan as you introduce it. Don't let that bother you. Some people don't like lectures, some don't like jokes, and some don't like simulations. You can't please all of the people all of the time, but you can achieve your purpose. That's why you should choose icebreakers and energizers carefully. Your icebreaker should be nonthreatening and relevant to the content. If participants are reluctant to participate, tell them the purpose and move on. Even if they do not participate, they will benefit from watching and listening to the other participants.

What's the most creative or effective icebreaker you know about?

....

....

....

....

....

Handout 3-8. Focus on What's Happening!

It's time to stop what you are doing and focus on what we have been doing through another lens. You have been observing this session through a participant's eyes. Now think of examining this session through the designer's eyes. Use a magnifying glass and consider all the details that have gone into the design. Think about what has been happening in the room from the designer's perspective. What have you noticed?

- What training techniques have been modeled?

- What trainer/facilitator skills did you observe?

- What design aspects have been incorporated?

- How has the trainer established a room conducive to learning?

- What's working?

- What's not working?

- What would you be doing right now if you were the trainer?

Handout 3-9. Activities: Countless Alternatives to Lecture

Activities come in many shapes and forms. Activities are important to your design because they are energizing, promote learning by doing, get participants to work together, and are motivational. How many learning methods can you name in each of these categories? List as many as you can.

Presentations refer to any method that gives information with less interaction than other methods (for example, panels, lecturettes, and debates):

....

Demonstrations typically involve someone showing the participants a process or modeling a procedure:

....

Reading refers to any method that pertains to interacting with the printed word:

....

Dramatization requires the participants or the facilitator to act out a role:

....

Discussions mean a two-way discussion that occurs between participants or between the facilitator and a participant:

....

Problem presentation and case are learning methods in which participants are presented with scenarios that require analysis or suggestions for improvement:

....

Art entails more creative methods involving drawing, design, sculpting, or other nonword events:

....

Play-likes are learning activities that are similar to dramatizations but less serious and more open ended:

....

Games refer to any board, card, television, computer, or physical event that leads to learning or review of the material:

....

Participant-directed refers to situations where participants take the leadership role in the delivery of training to others or the analysis of their own learning:

....

Participative events refers to icebreakers, energizers, and closers, ways for participants to get to know one another, recharge, and wind down:

....

Handout 3-10. Using KSAs for Instructional Design

Your learning objectives are the focus of your design, and you will refer to them throughout as your design begins to take shape to ensure that you are on the right path. Objectives fall into these three types of learning that you may have heard trainers shorten to the KSA abbreviation:

- **Knowledge** (K) involves the development of intellectual skills, such as understanding the principles of accounting, knowing the stages of childhood, understanding how interest rates affect the economy, or knowing how to get a book published.
- **Skills** (S) refers to physical movement, coordination, communication, use of motor skills, and demonstration of all soft skills. Examples of skills learning include the ability to use a digital camera, operate a backhoe, supervise staff, listen effectively, or kick a soccer ball.
- **Attitude** (A) refers to how we deal with things emotionally, such as feelings, motivation, and enthusiasm. Although attitude is not taught, it may affect an individual's performance. Trainers sometimes discuss whether it is the learner's "skill" or "will" that prevents top-notch performance. Trainers cannot change attitudes, but they frequently have the opportunity to influence attitudes.

This is based on Bloom's Taxonomy, which provides a way to understand the different types of learning that occur.

BLOOM'S TAXONOMY

In the early 1960s, Benjamin Bloom and a university committee identified three learning domains: cognitive, affective, and psychomotor. Trainers typically use knowledge (cognitive), skills (psychomotor), and attitude (affective) to describe the three categories of learning. You may think of the KSAs as the ultimate goals of the training process—what your learner will acquire as a result of training.

Bloom's committee expanded on the domains, creating a hierarchical ordering of the cognitive and affective learning outcomes. They subdivided each domain, starting from the simplest behavior to the most complex. This work is known as Bloom's Taxonomy. The divisions are not absolutes, and other systems and hierarchies have been developed. Bloom's Taxonomy, however, is easily understood and may be the most widely applied. Displayed here is an example of Bloom's Cognitive Domain. It displays the hierarchy of cognitive (knowledge) learning. Notice that as you move from left to right on the table, the verbs refer to more difficult tasks.

It is important to select the correct verb when you write your learning objectives.

Imitation	Manipulation	Precision	Articulation	Naturalization
Copy a model or pattern behavior	**Follow direction**	**Perfect original work**	**Adapt to unique situations**	**Natural ability and proficiency**
arrange	complete	devise	adjust	build
choose	compute	drive	calibrate	combine
copy	demonstrate	modify	construct	compose
describe	detect	operate	coordinate	create
duplicate	match	organize	detect	design
imitate	model	perfect	draw	initiate
isolate	move	refine	diagram	invent
relate	respond	repair	experiment	originate
select	reproduce	show		

Handout 3-11. Selecting Activities Based on the KSA

You will use different learning activities depending on the KSA (one of the three types of learning).

Select the type of learning (K, S, or A) that each activity would address best. There may be more than one for each activity.

Learning Method	Knowledge	Skill	Attitude
Lecturette			
Debate			
Group discussion			
Panel discussion			
Brainstorming			
Case study			
Role play			
Demonstration			
Demonstration with practice			
Independent study			
Field trip			
Film or video			
Simulation			
Game, exercise, or structured experience			
Handouts and print materials			
Hands-on practice			
Guided note taking			

In Focus: Vary Three for Interest

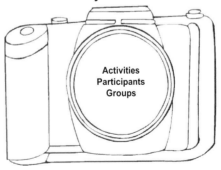

Activities
Participants
Groups

Handout 3-12. Developing Training Support Materials—Visuals

In general, when we think of support materials, we think of audiovisual materials, but you should also consider props, game pieces, demonstration materials, role-play cards, models, teasers, puzzles, and dozens of other things that will add excitement and interest to your training session.

Have you ever attended a session that used unusual items such as flashlights, paper bags, balloons, yarn, tape measures, peanut butter and jelly, ball and jacks, jump ropes, crayons, jelly beans, or chalk?

What's the most unusual item you've used in a training session?

....
....
....
....
....

CREATING POWERFUL POWERPOINT SLIDES

When you develop visuals such as PowerPoint slides or flipcharts, be sure that your materials are truly visual. PowerPoint slides are powerful when used to enhance your presentation. Never think of the PowerPoint as the presentation itself. Your slides should support the content you are delivering.

Keep It Simple: Use key words or ideas, keeping information concise. Aim for no more than three key concepts on each slide. Follow the 6 x 6 rule: Use no more than six lines vertically and six words across.

Use an Appropriate Font: Select a sans serif font, such as sans, Arial or Verdana, and choose a font size that can be seen by the person who will be seated the greatest distance from the screen. A font size of no less than 24 points should be used for general text; titles or headings should be 35 to 44 points. Generally, it is best to boldface the type.

Select a Visual Theme: Your audience has probably seen every template that is available from PowerPoint. Go online to find other PowerPoint designs, or create your own. Use color to enhance your theme, but use it judiciously. A light background with dark lettering is generally better than light on dark.

Add Interest: Use bullets, graphics, and layout to make your slides attractive. Something as simple as triangles instead of bullets adds a new twist. Remember that pictures say it best, and graphs explain numbers best. However, be careful not to overuse special effects like text or graphics that move. It may look like fun, but if it is overdone, it can be distracting and annoying to some members of your group. Use this only when appropriate or to help make your point.

Check for Accuracy: Give your slides to someone else to proof. Ensure that all information is complete, correct, and current.

Think of your visuals as support—support to help your learner stay focused and to keep you on track.

Visuals should accomplish three things. They should help your participants
- grasp the point quickly
- apply the concept to what they already know
- retain the information longer.

Handout 3-13. Know Your Training Style

You can assess training styles in many different ways. One way is to use the results of personality or behavioral assessments, such as the Myers-Briggs Type Indicator (MBTI) or the DISC (an acronym for dominance, influence, steadiness, and conscientiousness), to identify communication and other behavioral tendencies that relate to training.

You may also want to examine your own learning style to determine whether you have a bias as a trainer based on your own learning preferences. You can do this using an instrument such as the Personal Learning Styles Inventory or the Grasha-Riechmann Student Learning Style Scales. In this session, you will examine training style based on the roles that a trainer plays. Let's first examine the four dimensions of training.

THE FOUR DIMENSIONS OF TRAINING

A trainer focuses on four dimensions during a training session: content, process, task, and people. Most trainers attend to all four of these dimensions, and they may demonstrate a preference for one or two. These preferences can influence your perceived style of training. The four descriptions include examples of the ways a trainer attends to each dimension.

Content
The content is the purpose of the learning experience. A trainer focuses on content when he or she presents information or refers to materials or activities that contain information. You know a trainer is focusing on content if you hear phrases like "purpose for being here," "topics include," "information you'll need," or "other resources available include."

Process
This is the overall flow of a training program, as well as the flow of events within the program. Processes include such activities as facilitating discussion, forming small groups, and moving from one topic to another. You'll recognize a trainer who's focused on process if you hear "that discussion went well," "everything is going smoothly," or "we've lost continuity."

Task
These are all the things a trainer needs to do to manage a learning environment. These tasks may enable learning, such as setting up a simulation, or they may be purely administrative, such as record keeping. You may be able to tell that a trainer is task focused when he or she says things like, "I have to get this done before," "while you're on break, I'll be getting ready to," or "we'll have to stop this discussion and move on."

People
This dimension refers primarily to the participants and may include others related to the training program. Trainers focus on people when they do such things as modify the program to meet participant needs, encourage introductions and discussions, and schedule timely breaks. You'll know a trainer is focused on people when you hear phrases like "for your comfort," "you'll learn," and "I realize you want to . . . ."

Handout 3-14. Training Style Self-Assessment*

Rate the statements on a 1–5 scale: **1 = Not Like Me   3 = Neutral   5 = Most Like Me**

1. I like to verbally encourage participants to learn the most they can. ____

2. I provide a clear pathway so participants can learn the material on their own. ____

3. I make sure there is active participation between participants. ____

4. I enjoy being in front of the group. ____

5. I'm enthusiastic in a training setting because I think that my enthusiasm rubs off on participants. ____

6. I believe that it's enough to give people the information and materials with instructions so they can assume responsibility for their own learning. ____

7. In a training session, I believe it's more important to use small group and person-to-person interaction than lecture or individual exercises. ____

8. When I'm "on," I can influence the interest of participants significantly. ____

9. I believe every small success in learning should be positively reinforced. ____

10. I make sure each participant has time to think through the content. ____

11. I believe flexibility is critical to success when determining the order of activities in a training session. ____

12. It makes my day when participants give me positive feedback about my presentation. ____

13. I think participants see me as one of them. ____

14. I believe participants can get the most out of a training session by establishing and managing parameters for behavior and interaction. ____

15. All participants need many opportunities to add ideas during group discussions. ____

16. I believe that a good trainer needs to be able to explain content in a structured, logical way. ____

*Used with permission Biech, *Training for Dummies*, 2005

Handout 3-15. Training Style Self-Assessment Scoring

Examine the numbers you chose for each statement in handout 3-14. Determine the total for each of four styles.

1. Add the numbers for statements 1, 5, 9, 13 = _____ Preference for Coaching

2. Add the numbers for statements 2, 6, 10, 14 = _____ Preference for Guiding

3. Add the numbers for statements 3, 7, 11, 15 = _____ Preference for Facilitating

4. Add the numbers for statements 4, 8, 12, 16 = _____ Preference for Presenting

THE FOUR TRAINING STYLES

The grid in handout 3-16 presents the relationships among the four dimensions of training and how they create the four training styles. All four of the styles are critical to ensure a successful training session.

The **Coaching Style** is concerned with _____

The **Guiding Style** is concerned with _____

The **Facilitating Style** is concerned with _____

The **Presenting Style** is concerned with _____

In Focus: Four Training Styles

Coaching
Guiding
Facilitating
Presenting

Handout 3-16. Pulling It All Together

YOUR TRAINING PREFERENCES

The grid below demonstrates the relationship between all four dimensions of training. The perpendicular lines represent two continuums. At one end of the horizontal continuum is Content, and at the other end is Process. The vertical line is a continuum that represents the disparity between a focus on Task and a focus on People. Remember that trainers may show a preference for attending to one training dimension more than the other.

Task

Presenting   Guiding

Content   Process

Coaching   Facilitating

People

Handout 3-17. **Understand Your Training Style**

Understanding your training style helps you to identify the effectiveness of your current instructional style. Trainers are most effective when they help adult learners progress through the steps in the adult learning process.

Training style is something that each instructor develops from personal experience. To be more effective, different training styles are useful for presenting different types of content and responding to different learning styles. Because individuals learn differently, a skilled trainer will take this into consideration and will vary the training style.

Trainers generally have a preferred training style. An excellent trainer will be aware of all training styles and will match the style required to the learner and the situation. Trainers can be more effective by developing lesser-used styles and avoiding the overuse of a preferred style. It's all about balance!

PUTTING STYLE INTO PRACTICE

1. What does your Training Style Self-Assessment tell you about your preferences? Are you balanced in your use of all four roles, or do you have strong preferences toward one or two of them?

....

....

....

....

....

....

....

2. What insights have you gained by thinking about this activity?

....

....

....

....

....

....

....

3. Where are your areas for growth?

....

....

....

....

....

....

....

Handout 3-18. Help! I've Been Asked to Conduct a Webinar!

What if you are conducting a webinar or some other e-learning event? Although each type of technology is different, here are a few ideas for preparation of a webinar:

- **Select the date and time.** It should be no less than six weeks prior to the webinar. Research shows that the best days of the week are Tuesday, Wednesday, or Thursday. In the United States, the best time is between 12:00 p.m. and 2:00 p.m. (EST).
- **Send invitations.** It appears that email is the best way to invite people to a webinar. Notices in newsletters, links to websites, or press releases are much less effective.
- **Respond immediately.** When participants begin to register for the event, send a response and the guidelines immediately so that you maintain the momentum.
- **Give an online orientation.** If you anticipate first-time users, this might be useful. An orientation to online learning could include having them do a systems check the day before; providing written instructions for chat, posting, and asking questions; demonstrating each tool with an early activity; or even asking a polling question early to get them started.
- **Design your webinar.** Plan for a 30- to 60-minute session. Create objectives, and plan your delivery matrix. The maximum number of objectives for this session should be three. Allow time at the end for questions from the participants.
- **Develop a compelling PowerPoint presentation.** Make the slides visually interesting. Use one color scheme, and add variety with graphs, clip art, or photos. Dark text on a light background is easier to read, and red text should be avoided completely. Put a small amount of text on each slide; use the 6 x 6 rule (maximum of six lines of text, with six words in each line), just as you would for any other PowerPoint presentation.
- **Keep your PowerPoint file size small.** This benefits those who may use a dial-up connection. For example, avoid color gradients, and ensure that your slides are 10" by 7.5", sized for an on-screen show.
- **Design to keep participants engaged.** Use the interactive web-conferencing features available, such as polling, chatting, quizzes, or surveys, to keep participants involved. Use the whiteboard feature for brainstorming or creating drawings.
- **Plan for Q&A.** Prepare for the kinds of questions you anticipate. You may even plant a question in the group to encourage other participants to speak up.
- **Practice.** Rehearse your presentation several times. Schedule a complete dry run with your conference provider to be sure you are comfortable with the platform.
- **Rehearse the production portion.** Include the logistics during your rehearsal, for example, introductions, transitions and handoffs, and know who will be where.
- **Use the telephone handset.** This will provide the best audio quality during the session. A speakerphone or cell phone does not provide the best quality.
- **Maintain a studio-like atmosphere.** Post a "Do Not Disturb" sign, eliminate background noise, turn cell phones off, mute your computer, and close email.
- **Follow up immediately.** Acknowledge all registrants by email. For those who attended, send a thank-you note and instructions for how to access the archive of the event. Send a "sorry we missed you" note to any who registered but did not attend. You may also want to ask for feedback.

These ideas certainly do not cover everything, but they will get you started. It is important that activities are well thought out and interaction is designed into the session; this is not the time to be spontaneous. You might ask someone whom you know will be on the webinar to contribute to a certain content area.

Technical difficulties create another challenge, and that's why you will most likely have technical support. The most common problem is that participants have forgotten to get their password or have forgotten how to sign in. You can reduce this challenge by asking everyone to sign in at least 10 minutes before the session begins. Ask a colleague to assist with technical difficulties, gather questions, and offer general support.

A more personal challenge is getting to know the participant as a person. It is difficult to determine the participants' learning style or to assist with specific concerns. When listening, it is hard to hear the content and even harder to hear the intent of the message. Even with the obvious challenges, webinars fill a training need. Your preparation and practice is even more critical using this training venue.

Handout 3-19. Focus on You—Wrap-Up of Module 3

1. What is the most important thing you have learned in this module?

   ....

   ....

   ....

   ....

2. What will you implement or change as a result of what you have learned?

   ....

   ....

   ....

   ....

3. What resources will you require to do what you would like?

   ....

   ....

   ....

   ....

4. Who could help you?

   ....

   ....

   ....

   ....

5. What questions do you have that need answers?

   ....

   ....

   ....

   ....

Handout 4-1. Introduction to Module 4—Implement and Facilitate

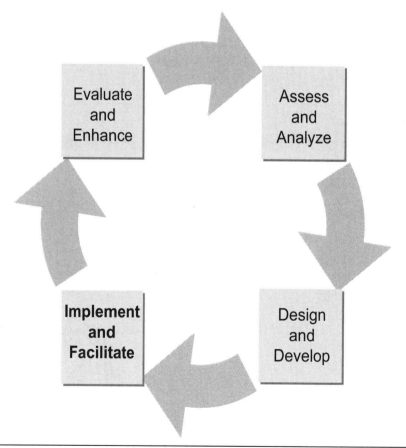

IMPLEMENT AND FACILITATE MODULE OBJECTIVES

By the end of this module, you will be able to
- discuss different learning styles
- establish a positive learning environment
- evaluate effective presentation skills
- list advantages and disadvantages of lecturettes
- use visuals appropriately
- recall techniques to manage nervousness
- resolve problem classroom situations
- ask and answer questions that lead to learning.

Handout 4-2. How Do You Address Different Learning Styles in the Classroom?

How do you learn? Hear? See? Do you also touch? Smell? Taste, too? We gain information through our five senses. Most information comes through seeing and hearing. Learning style experts like David Kolb and Ned Herrmann present models for how each of us learns.

Kolb's research, for example, shows that effective learners need these four kinds of learning abilities: concrete experience, reflective observation, abstract conceptualization, and active experimentation. He believes that each of us relies on some abilities more than others and produces four learning styles: the converger, the diverger, the assimilator, and the accommodator. His model is appealing because it explains how people learn in all situations, not just in educational settings.

W.E. (Ned) Herrmann's research focuses on the brain because it is the central processor of all learning activities. Herrmann's whole brain model explains brain specialization in each of the four quadrants and that each quadrant has its own preferred way of learning. Herrmann's model explains the four preferences in learning styles, but it recognizes that we often zigzag around the model when we learn. The result is a belief that the most successful approach to learning, design, and delivery of training is to create a whole brain experience for a learning group.

AUDITORY, VISUAL, AND KINESTHETIC LEARNERS

Referring to the first sentence on this page, one of the easiest ways to consider learning style is to think about our senses and how we take in information. You (and your learners) use your brain's hundred billion cells to process information in a variety of ways. Most of us have a preferred style for learning. We also have a secondary style.

Although it's true that we learn through all of our senses, these three are more dominant:
- auditory (hearing)
- visual (seeing)
- kinesthetic (physically experiencing).

WHAT'S YOUR STYLE?

Take the quick quiz here to determine your preferred style. Place a check mark in front of the statements that best describe you. Turn the page to determine your primary and secondary preferences.

1. I like to read books.
2. I take many notes during classes.
3. I frequently need to have verbal directions repeated.
4. I read maps and follow written directions well.
5. I like to doodle and sketch pictures.
6. I like to talk on the phone.
7. I like to write.
8. I prefer to talk about a topic than to read about it.
9. I remember stories and jokes; I can repeat conversations word for word.
10. I prefer books on tape to reading.
11. I like games and role plays.
12. I expend nervous energy by tapping fingers or playing with objects.
13. I use hands when I talk.
14. I like to touch or feel things when I learn about them.
15. I like tasks that require me to take things apart or put them together.

continued on next page

Handout 4-2. How Do You Address Different Learning Styles in the Classroom? *continued*

Use this guide to identify the three learning style preference statements:
- Visual: Statements 1–5
- Auditory: Statements 6–10
- Kinesthetic: Statements 11–15.

What are your primary and secondary learning style preferences? If you have rated two styles equally, you probably shift between the two, depending upon the situation.

As a trainer, it's important to recognize your preferred learning style:
- It ensures that you consciously design content that is balanced to all styles.
- It reminds you when you deliver content that the learners in your room may not all learn like you do.
- It helps you recognize other styles and assist individuals with their learning.

So What's a Trainer to Do?

It's important to present content in the way that's easiest for your learners to comprehend. Unfortunately, it is highly unlikely that you will have a group of participants who will all have the same learning style.

Each of your participants will have an individual learning style. Remember that there are different theories about how humans learn best, and each theory is different. All theorists agree, however, that individuals do learn differently. Great trainers take this into consideration when they design and deliver training programs.

So, what do you do? Do what all good trainers do:
- Accept that people learn differently.
- Recognize that each learning style has a preference for one method over another.
- When you design or deliver training, create a variety of approaches that will use techniques and activities that address all preferences.

Identify ways that you could address each of these learning styles as you facilitate a training session. How might your plans change for an e-learning experience?

Visual:

....

....

....

Auditory:

....

....

....

Kinesthetic:

....

....

....

Handout 4-3. How Do You Establish a Positive Learning Environment?

We opened this train-the-trainer session by stating that you need to focus on the learners. It is your job as the trainer to use whatever you have at your disposal to establish a learning environment of trust, respect, safety, integrity, and success.

CREATE A SAFE HAVEN FOR LEARNING

Some learners may arrive excited about the training. Others may think that training is punishment, and others may bring burdens with them. You can create a safe haven. Here are some ideas:
- Be prepared early enough to greet participants at the door, welcome them, learn their names, and allow time for them to tell you something about themselves.
- Share the objectives of the training early, prior to the session if possible.
- Let participants know how they will benefit from the information.
- Demonstrate your respect for each individual.
- Add whimsy to pique curiosity, and add a smile; for example, use crayons, clay, or brightly colored sticky notes.
- Use names and sincere reinforcement to build rapport.

CREATE A COMFORTABLE ENVIRONMENT

Arrive in a training room early enough to make it yours so that you can welcome the learners as your guests. To create a comfortable environment, consider these ideas:
- Make sure that lighting is bright. It's depressing to walk into a ballroom when the lights are dimmed.
- Learn how to adjust the thermostat to the level that is most comfortable for the majority of the participants. Remember that you will never please everyone all the time. Do your best.
- Ensure that the environment feels comfortable. Hide empty boxes, straighten chairs, and place materials neatly at each seat. When the room is in order, people feel that you took the time and trouble to prepare for them.
- Ensure that you and your visuals can be seen and heard by all learners. Try it out.
- Have coffee ready in the morning, and plan for ample breaks.

ENCOURAGE PARTICIPATION

Active and ample participation is the most important thing you can encourage to enhance learning. Here are a couple of thoughts to get you started:
- Use small breakout groups to overcome early reluctance to share ideas or concerns.
- Use body language to encourage participation; positive nods, smiles, and eye contact all show that you are interested in others' ideas.
- Share something about yourself to begin a trusted exchange of ideas.
- Learn techniques to get learners to open up.

FACILITATE MORE THAN YOU PRESENT

A straight lecturette is rarely required, perhaps only when rules or laws must be imparted word for word. Facilitating, rather than lecturing, usually enhances learning for everyone. Here are some ideas:
- Create discussion. Not just between you and the learners, but among the learners.
- Get opinions and ideas out in the open before you deliver your message. You may be surprised at how much training the learners can do for you.
- Provide opportunities for participants to evaluate their own learning throughout the session.
- Create experiential learning activities in which the learners discover their own "aha!" moments.

ENCOURAGE PARTICIPANTS TO TRACK THEIR OWN PROGRESS

Tracking progress means celebrating success, overcoming obstacles, and deciding next steps.
Plan for ways participants can do this:
- Create individual checkpoints in the program.

continued on next page

Handout 4-3. How Do You Establish a Positive Learning Environment? *continued*

- Build in group review of learning.
- Encourage participants to identify barriers to the learning.
- Pair individuals as sounding boards for one another.
- Plan celebrations: distributing certificates, team applauses, or "moments in the sun."

Room Set-Up Your room setup also establishes a positive learning environment. What are you trying to accomplish in your training session? Are you trying to build teams, build one large team, or interject cooperation?

Listed below are several seating arrangements. Can you think of a specific time when you might use each one during the training sessions that you currently conduct?

ARRANGEMENT	GROUP SIZE	ADVANTAGES	DISADVANTAGES
U-Shaped	12–22	Encourages large group discussion; builds the larger team; encourages close contact with participants	If a small room, may be difficult to work with those on the other side; linear layout makes eye contact among participants difficult
V-Shaped (V points to front)	Teams of 4–5 and groups of 16–25	Easy to work in table teams; no one's back is entirely facing back of room; best alternative using rectangular tables	Some difficulty to promote teamwork among the entire group
Clusters	16–50	Promotes teamwork in each cluster; everyone faces the front if chairs are on one side only	Difficult to get participation from those who face the back; some participants may need to move chairs to face the front
Single Round/Square	8–12	Facilitates problem solving; smaller size promotes total involvement; easy for trainer to step out of the action	Media and visual use is difficult; limited group size
Conference	8–12	Moderate communication among group	Maintains trainer as lead; sense of formality; inability for trainer to get close to participants
Classroom	Any size	Traditional, may be expected by learners; trainer controls; participants can view visuals	Low involvement; one-way communication; difficult to form small groups

Handout 4-4. Focus on What's Happening!

It's time to stop what you are doing and focus on what we have been doing through another lens. You have been observing this session through a participant's eyes. Now think about examining this session through the designer's eyes. Use a magnifying glass and consider all the details that have gone into the design. Think about what has been happening in the room from the designer's perspective. What have you noticed?

- What training techniques have been modeled?
- What trainer/facilitator skills have been used?
- What design aspects have been incorporated?
- How has the trainer established a room conducive to learning?
- What's working?
- What's not working?
- What would you be doing right now if you were the trainer?

Handout 4-5. Presenting a Dynamic Delivery

A quote that should guide your presentations is, "A good speech is less about what they say, and all about what we hear and what we see. "You could be delivering fascinating information, but if you are using a monotone voice, including lots of fillers, and playing with your marker, it will be almost impossible for your participants to learn.

PARTICIPANTS	WHAT IS GOOD?	WHAT NEEDS TO CHANGE?
What They Hear		
What They See		

USE NOTES TO KEEP YOUR DELIVERY ORGANIZED

Notes should be considered as a guide to keep you on track and on time. How can you use notes effectively? Here are some thoughts:

- Practice with your notes. They should become a support system that you know well and rely on.
- Learn to hold your notes comfortably and unobtrusively. You'll need to tape yourself or present in front of a full-length mirror to decide what works for you and how you look best.
- Use a "speak and peek" process, meaning that you continue to speak while you peek briefly at your notes.
- Don't fold or staple your notes. Folding weakens the paper and makes the pages prone to flop over as you are holding them. A staple prevents your flexibility. In addition, you'll appear more professional if you do not need to flip the page over as if you are holding some long bill of lading.
- Be sure the pages are clearly numbered so that they are easy to put back in order.
- Find ways to cue yourself about where to look for specific information on your notes. Possibilities include highlighting, underlining, and using a different color of marker or font.

Handout 4-6. What Are the Pros and Cons of Lectures?

Lecturettes are short spurts of information, generally interspersed with humor and short activities. Although you will often use activities to maximize participation, there are still times when you must deliver information.

DISADVANTAGES OF LECTURES	ADVANTAGES OF LECTURES

INCREASE PARTICIPATION—EVEN WHEN YOU LECTURE!

Try some of these suggestions to encourage participation, even when you must deliver information:
- Design pop quizzes in the middle of the lecturette.
- Ask questions about predictions or recall of information.
- Create a conversation between the trainer and the participants.
- Intersperse demonstrations.
- Develop a page of guided note taking in the form of questions or fill in the blanks.
- Develop key word outlines of the presentation, leaving room to add additional ideas.
- Use visuals to go with the lecturette, so participants can follow your words visually.
- Stop at several points along the way to ask if everyone is with you.
- Design a partial story at the beginning and complete the story at the end of the lecturette.
- Find ways to interject humor, such as creating a cartoon to match the content.

Handout 4-7. Do You Get Nervous?

Nervousness is nothing more than a fear reflex. It is natural, and it occurs because your body is getting ready for fight or flight. Nervousness may be displayed in numerous ways: pacing or swaying, fidgeting with a pen, jingling change in your pocket, perspiring, shaking, clearing your throat, grimacing, tenseness, and dozens of other things. Nevertheless, if you have interesting content, your participants will never notice that you are nervous.

The number one rule regarding nervousness is, "Do not tell your participants that you are nervous." If you don't tell them, chances are your participants will never know! Here are some tips to address your nervousness:

- Recognize that you will be nervous. Know your signs of nervousness and then say, "Oh there it is—that butterfly in my stomach. That's my nervous signal. "Then move on.
- Find the best way to relax before you begin. It might be a couple of head or shoulder rolls, a few isometric exercises, or deep breathing. Do what works best for you.
- Arrive early, to take ownership of the training room. When your "guests" arrive, it will be as if you are on your home field.
- Wear clothes that you feel great in. Avoid a new suit, new shoes, or a new haircut.
- Organize yourself. In fact, put your organizational skills into overdrive. It will relax you to know that everything is where it belongs and is ready to go.
- Got a security blanket? Use it. Maybe it is a glass of water. Besides, the water is handy for a dry throat or when you need a pause to remember what you were saying!
- Tell yourself that your participants want you to succeed. Send yourself positive messages, "I've got this covered! It's going to be grrreeaaat!"
- Get participants involved early. You could ask a question, start a discussion, or organize an activity. After that, it will feel more like a two-way conversation.

Remember that even if you are nervous, your participants will rarely notice it unless you tell them, and then they will start looking for the signs. If you focus on your participants and their needs, you take the attention away from yourself and get over the butterflies fluttering in your stomach sooner. Remember that nervousness is natural. Try the techniques listed below to address specific nervous symptoms.

IDEAS FOR SPECIFIC NERVOUS SYMPTOMS

These ideas do not remove the nervousness, but they may mask it or provide you with a temporary crutch:

Shakiness	Stand near a table and use it as a touchstone; avoid caffeine.
Moving/swaying	Plant your feet a full shoulder's width apart.
Trembling legs	Don't try to control; isolate the muscles and shake out before you begin.
Sweaty palms	Try talc or antiperspirant (experiment with it first).
Squeaky voice	No iced beverages; try lemon and honey in warm decaffeinated tea. Try "Throat Coat," a commercial tea.
Throat mucus	Lemon in warm tea; avoid dairy products.
Dry throat	Bite on a lemon or use a mouth freshener; have water available.
Fillers	Write a large "UM" on your notes to remind you not to say it; good eye contact.
Facial expressions	Greet people early and think of them as your friends.
Jangle change	Empty your pockets.
Flushed skin	Wear red or darker colors to camouflage it.
Fast pulse rate	Breath deeply.
Twitching	Experiment between training sessions; try rubbing or tapping area.
Rapid speech	Write a cue to "slow down" on your notes; practice pausing.

What works for you? ....

Handout 4-8. Presentation Tools Demonstration

Develop a three-minute presentation that displays all the things you could do incorrectly with one of these audiovisual tools:
- LCD projector
- whiteboard
- flipchart
- participant handouts
- DVD/CD player
- other.

What can you do?

....

....

....

....

....

Suggestions for Appropriate Use of Visuals

MEDIA/SUPPORT	TIPS FOR USING
LCD Projector	
Whiteboard	
Flipcharts	
Participant Manuals, Handouts	
DVD/CD, Movies	
Others	

Handout 4-9. The Quandary Queue

Have you ever had one of those days? You know the kind of day where everything goes wrong. You woke up ill, and when you arrived, your equipment did not work. Your participants all seem to be on another planet, their responses are incorrect or out of context, and the method you are using is obviously not working. You spent more time with one section, thereby shortchanging another. You've lost the attention of the group, and now the fire alarm goes off! What do you do?

What quandaries and challenges do you face in the classroom, and how do you handle them? Queue them up here:

....

....

....

....

....

....

ANY DIFFICULT PARTICIPANTS?

What kinds of difficult or inappropriate behaviors have you addressed? What works?

GENERAL GUIDELINES

- Begin by ignoring the behavior.
- Stop the behavior if it is disruptive to others, but keep your cool; don't take it personally.
- These strategies sometimes work:
  - Stop talking until the behavior ends.
  - Use nonverbal cues, such as talking between a side conversation, holding up your hand.
  - Refer to the ground rules if appropriate.
  - Directly ask for the behavior to stop or change.
  - Take a break.
  - Discuss the behavior with the individual at a break.
- Continue to respect the individual; consider that perhaps the participant does not realize that he or she is disruptive.
- Keep the participant involved because you don't want him or her to disengage.
- Maintain the involvement of the rest of the group. They want you to succeed and will judge how you handle the situation.

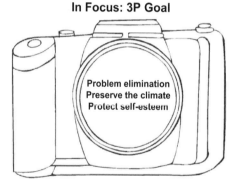

In Focus: 3P Goal

Problem elimination
Preserve the climate
Protect self-esteem

PREPARE TO PREVENT PROBLEMS

The key to handling difficulties in a training session is preparation and prevention. Unfortunately, no matter how thoroughly you prepare, things will still go wrong. Smile and keep it in perspective.

Handout 4-10. Skill Practice Delivery Preparation

If you want to learn a skill, you need to practice. For example, to learn about the game of tennis, you can do these things:

- Read a brochure about the rules and how to keep score.
- Read a book about the history of tennis.
- Talk to someone about where the big tournaments are held.
- Watch a demonstration on a DVD for the proper grip and serve.
- Observe several matches to learn where the players stand.
- Practice hitting the ball against a wall to learn eye-hand coordination.

All of these things are helpful, but to learn the game of tennis, you really need to play the game and practice.

Let's take some time now to practice the game of training:

- Select one of the resources provided.
- Prepare a 10-minute presentation based on one topic from the publication.
- The topic should be new to you.
- Plan your presentation with a beginning, a middle, and an end.
- Write a learning objective.
- Build in interaction and participation.
- Plan to use at least one visual support (flipchart, handout, prop, or PowerPoint).
- The checklist in handout 4-11 will be used for the rest of your small group members to provide feedback to you.
- Decide what kind of feedback you would like to receive. Tell your small group before your presentation so that they can tell you what they observed.
- The facilitator has supplies for you such as flipcharts, index cards, paper, or markers.

You have time to prepare now. You will have an additional 30 minutes prior to your presentation to finalize it.

Handout 4-11. Training/Facilitating Checklist

Use this checklist to provide feedback to your colleagues. Consider it a guide only. You are not expected to respond to every item for every person.

SKILLS	COMMENTS
How effectively did the trainer...	
Facilitate Learning: Provide an effective introduction? Use appropriate group facilitation techniques? Use a visual aid skillfully? Use an appropriate pace? Debrief activities? Stay focused on the topic?	
Create a Positive Learning Environment: Make the learning interesting? Use relevant examples? Provide honest feedback? Handle incorrect answers appropriately?	
Encourage Participation: Establish rapport? Make eye contact with all participants? Appear relaxed and pleasant? Use encouraging body language? Provide reinforcement for participation? Exhibit nonjudgmental behaviors?	
Communicate Content and Process: Provide an organized delivery? Summarize clearly? Encourage questions? Listen well? Use appropriate nonverbal communication? Speak and enunciate clearly? Project voice effectively? Use appropriate humor? Deliver constructive feedback?	
Ensure Learning Outcomes: Assess individual learning? Provide time for Q&A? Encourage on-the-job application? Use relevant examples?	

continued on next page

Handout 4-11. Training/Facilitating Checklist, *continued*

SKILLS	COMMENTS
Establish Credibility: Demonstrate understanding of the content? Display confidence? Maintain composure? Describe personal experiences? Answer questions? **Additional Comments?**	

Handout 4-12. Questions, Questions, From All Perspectives

GETTING PARTICIPANTS TO ASK QUESTIONS

- Tell participants that you encourage their questions.
- Stop at natural points in your presentation and ask for questions.
- Pause long enough for participants to formulate questions.
- Give signals such as, "Let's pause here so you can ask questions." Then wait for questions.
- Watch facial expressions; if a participant looks puzzled, stop and ask if he or she has a question.
- If two or more participants are talking among themselves, ask if there is something they would like clarified.
- Allow time for participants to ask their questions privately. They may be too shy to ask in front of the group.

TIPS FOR ASKING QUESTIONS

- Plan some questions in advance.
- Increase participation by including questions early in the session.
- Know why you are including questions: to create discussion, introduce controversy, correct response, review information, or hear hypothetical comments.
- Keep questions short.
- Know whether you want opinions or information.
- Consider whether it should be an open-ended question.
- If asking a direct question, say the participant's name first, and then ask the question.
- Pause for answers.
- Use follow-up questions to further clarify or expand the initial response.
- Paraphrase responses, especially when the response was not focused.
- Use a round-robin if you want to hear from everyone.

TIPS FOR ANSWERING QUESTIONS

- Anticipate participants' questions.
- Inform participants of your expectations early in the session.
- Paraphrase questions to ensure that everyone heard and understood the question.
- Ask for clarification if necessary.
- Be brief.
- "I don't know, but I will find out," is a perfectly good response.
- Redirect questions or encourage other responses from the entire group.
- If the question is not relevant, invite the participant to discuss it at a break.
- Avoid showing your feelings to a hostile questioner.
- Reword hostile questions.
- Include the entire audience in your response with body position and eye contact.

Handout 4-13. How Do You Bring Closure to a Training Session?

An exceptional trainer takes the time to end appropriately.

Opening your training session requires focus; closing your session does, too. Too often training sessions just end. There is a flurry of activity to complete the evaluation, to catch planes, and to get ahead of the rush-hour traffic. Plan your ending as carefully as you plan your opening.

WHAT TO ACCOMPLISH

- Ensure that expectations were met.
- Allow time for individuals to set goals and make final plans.
- Summarize the accomplishments and gain commitment to action.
- Bring closure to the experience with a final group experience.
- Send them off with a final encouraging word or two.

What ideas do you have for implementing these closing steps?

....

....

....

....

....

....

....

....

....

....

....

....

....

....

....

....

Finally, stand by the door and say good-bye to each individual. Shake their hands, wish them luck, and offer follow-up, as appropriate. You owe it to your participants to provide the best training session ever. Make it the best it can be from start to finish.

End with a bang—not a fizzle!

Handout 4-14. Focus on You—Wrap-Up of Module 4

1. What is the most important thing you have learned in this module?

....

....

....

....

....

2. What will you implement or change as a result of what you have learned?

....

....

....

....

....

3. What resources will you require to do what you would like?

....

....

....

....

....

4. Who could help you?

....

....

....

....

....

5. What questions do you have that need answers?

....

....

....

....

....

Handout 5-1. Introduction to Module 5—Evaluate and Enhance

EVALUATE AND ENHANCE MODULE OBJECTIVES

By the end of this module, you will be able to
- explain Kirkpatrick's four levels of evaluation
- discuss the ROI for training efforts
- establish a personal development plan for your continuous learning.

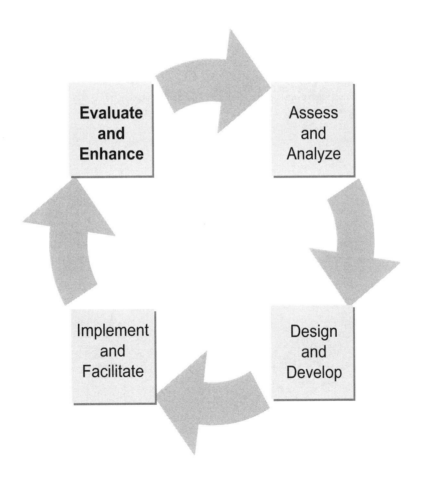

Handout 5-2. The Importance of Evaluation

Evaluate and Enhance is the final module of this train-the-trainer session, and Evaluate is the final phase of the ADDIE model. You can step back and view the beauty of the entire model.

The evaluation stage is important to you as a trainer. It is here so that you can prove your value as a business partner to your organization. You can answer these questions:

- How has training changed employee performance?
- How has training increased sales or reduced expenses?
- How has training reduced rework and defects?
- How has training affected turnover and employee satisfaction?
- And ultimately, how is training affecting the bottom line?

Evaluation is the ADDIE phase that ensures that training or other performance solutions are meeting the needs of learners and organizations as a whole.

This module will give you a chance to review Kirkpatrick's four levels of evaluation and to explore Phillips's ROI model.

Evaluation is beneficial only if it is used to enhance the next training, affect how changes are implemented, and make decisions about how to constantly improve.

Finally, evaluation should also pertain to you, the trainer. Evaluating your progress and your next steps for improvement should be foremost in your mind. After all, that is why you are attending this train-the-trainer session, right?

Handout 5-3. Evaluating Progress

In the first column of the table, identify all the things that you could measure to determine progress; some of these things may or may not occur as a result of attending this train-the-trainer session. In the second column, list the ways you could measure it.

WHAT COULD YOU MEASURE?	HOW WOULD YOU MEASURE IT?

Handout 5-4. Kirkpatrick's Four Levels of Evaluation

Your focus is to improve your participants' skills and knowledge. Evaluation allows you to determine whether there has been any improvement. Evaluation can also determine the cost-benefit of the program. It can track participant progress, identify future participants, and determine the strengths and weaknesses of the training process. Kirkpatrick's four levels of evaluation can help you to design an evaluation plan.

When should you begin thinking about what you want to evaluate?

....

....

....

Level 1: Reaction. Focuses on the participants' reaction to or satisfaction with the program and frequently includes how the participants plan to apply what they have learned. Sometimes called "happy sheets," most training efforts are evaluated at this level.

How do you measure this level?

....

....

....

Level 2: Learning. Indicates what participants have absorbed and whether they know how to implement what they learned. Tests, skill practices, simulations, group evaluations, role plays and other assessment tools are used to determine what participants learned.

How do you measure this level?

....

....

....

Level 3: Behavior. Focuses on changes in on-the-job behavior, that is, whether the participants apply what they have learned and transfer it to the workplace. Measures may include the frequency and use of skills.

How do you measure this level?

....

....

....

Level 4: Results. Measurements focus on the actual impact on the business as participants successfully apply the program material. Typical measures might include output, quality, time, costs, and customer satisfaction.

How do you measure this level?

....

....

....

Handout 5-5. Why Return-on-Investment?

Many organizations now add a fifth level of evaluation for return-on-investment (ROI). Jack Phillips is considered to be one of the early proponents of this evaluation level. ROI compares the monetary benefits of the training program with the cost of the program. Although ROI can be expressed several ways, it is typically presented as a benefit-cost ratio.

ROI is important to you as a trainer because it is one place where you may demonstrate your value as a business partner.

How Do You Measure ROI?

The ROI process consists of five steps. Note that Kirkpatrick's Level 1 through Level 4 are essential for gathering the initial data.

1. **Collect post-program data**. A variety of methods may be used to collect data, similar to the ways you collect data for Level 1 through Level 4.
2. **Isolate the effects of training.** Many factors may influence performance data; therefore, steps must be taken to pinpoint the amount of improvement that can be attributed directly to the training program. A comprehensive set of tools is used that may include a control group, trend line analysis, forecasting models, and impact estimates from various groups.
3. **Convert data to a monetary value.** Assess the Level 4 data and assign a monetary value. Techniques might include using historical costs, using salaries and benefits as value for time, converting output to profit contributions, or using external databases.
4. **Tabulate program costs.** Identify the program costs, which include the cost to design and develop the program and materials, facilitator salary, facilities, travel, administrative and overhead costs, and the cost of participants to attend the program.
5. **Calculate the ROI.** The ROI is calculated by dividing the net program benefits (program benefits less program costs) by the program costs, multiplied by 100. In this step, you will also identify intangible benefits, such as increased job satisfaction, improved customer service, or reduced complaints.

Although it feels like a great deal of work, measuring ROI will be worth it if you need to provide evidence to management about the value of training.

Benefits of Measuring ROI

Probably the most important benefit of measuring ROI is to respond to management's question of whether training adds value to the organization. The ROI calculations convince management that training is an investment, not an expense. The ROI analysis also provides information about specific training programs, which ones contributed the most to the bottom line, which ones need to be improved, and which ones are an expense to the organization. When the training practitioner acts on this data, the process has the added benefit of improving the effectiveness of all training programs.

ROI provides an essential aspect of the entire evaluation process.

When you evaluate training, be sure you know what you want to measure and how you might collect the data to isolate the impact of the program. You may want to measure both ROI and intangible benefits.

Handout 5-6. Evaluate and Enhance

The evaluation phase of ADDIE, in addition to supporting the ROI of training, requires that you use the evaluation information to enhance, improve, or perhaps completely revamp the training design in some cases.

Evaluation is the final phase in the training cycle, but it is certainly only the beginning of improving training. It will be up to you to take your training efforts to the next level, relying on the evaluation to help you decide what to improve. In Don Kirkpatrick's words, "Evaluation is a science and an art. It is a blend of concepts, theory, principles, and techniques. It is up to you to do the application."

EVALUATING AND ENHANCING YOU

This phase is not just for the training; it is meant for you too. Before you plan how you will enhance your own skills and continue to learn, check these ideas to get you started:

- Polish your presentation skills by joining Toastmasters International or taking a presentation skills course. We all get rusty and pick up habits we may not be aware of.
- Maintain membership in professional organizations. Although ASTD is the one place you can turn to for cutting-edge information in the field, consider others as well: Instructional Systems Association (ISA), International Society for Performance Improvement (ISPI), Society for Human Resource Management (SHRM), or National Speakers Association (NSA).
- Read journals, magazines, and books. Your reading selections should encompass the workplace learning and performance field, of course, but they should also delve into the industry that you serve so that you will be better prepared to support the organization(s) for which you provide training.
- Subscribe to newsletters in your field as a good source of current information. Check some that are available online.
- Attend conferences, seminars, professional chapter meetings, and other presentations. ASTD's International Conference & Expo (ICE) should be considered one of your key growth events, not just to gain knowledge from the sessions, but also as a networking opportunity.
- Establish your personal networking team to whom you can turn for advice, suggestions, assistance, and knowledge.
- Check for online information and services.
- Stay current with the latest research in training, as well as in the industry you serve.
- Try one new thing each time you develop or deliver a training program.
- If you haven't already, begin to apply more of a human performance improvement (HPI) approach where the focus is on results.
- Identify the next workshop that is right for you.

In Focus: 3Cs of a Great Trainer

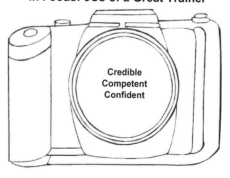

**Credible
Competent
Confident**

Handout 5-7.   Focus on You—Wrap-Up of Module 5

1. Review this module and look back at the "Focus on You" pages after modules 1, 2, 3, and 4. Evaluate what you have learned and what you still need to learn. Summarize those items here.

....

....

....

2. What are the most important things you have learned about training?

....

....

....

3. What are the most important things you have learned about yourself?

....

....

....

4. What will you implement or change as a result of what you have learned? Capture your ideas in this action plan.

OBJECTIVES	STRATEGIES	WHO WILL HELP ME	RESOURCES REQUIRED	REVIEW DATE

Handout 5-8. Congratulations to Me!

1. Design a congratulations card for yourself (see next page). Focus on how you will answer these questions two months from now:
   - What will you have accomplished based on the train-the-trainer session?

   ....

   ....

   ....

   - What goals have you completed?

   ....

   ....

   ....

   - What have you done that deserves congratulations?

   ....

   ....

   ....

2. Review your action plan to identify something that you want to focus on doing better. List it here.

   ....

   ....

   ....

   ....

   ....

3. Complete your card:
   - Use the markers and crayons to decorate your card on the next page.
   - Sign your card and insert it in the envelope.
   - Address it to yourself, and we will mail it back for your review in eight weeks.

continued on next page

Handout 5-8. Congratulations to Me!, *continued*

Congratulations _____

(Your name)

It is so exciting that you have

_____

and

_____

Keep Up the Great Work!

Appendix—Using the Accompanying Compact Disc

Using the Compact Disc—General

Contents of the Compact Disc

You will find the handouts and other tools and support material masters referenced throughout this workbook on the accompanying CD:

- participant handouts
- PowerPoint slides
- Session at a Glance (tables 1–5, one for each module)
- Trainer's Guide (chapters 5–9)
- flipchart preparation and flipcharts (for modules 3 and 4)
- "Team 2 Notes" memo for activity 2-6
- pairwise card set for activity 3-2
- equipment and materials packing list (also see chapter 4)
- table tent
- train-the-trainer evaluations (2)
- train-the-trainer certificates (2).

To access any of these files, insert the CD and click on the appropriate file name.

Computer Requirements

All of the files can be used on a variety of computer platforms.

To read or print the .pdf files included on the CD, Adobe Acrobat Reader software must be installed on your system. This program can be downloaded free of cost from the Adobe website, www.adobe.com.

To use or adapt the contents of the PowerPoint presentation files on the CD, Microsoft PowerPoint software must be installed on your system. If you just want to view the PowerPoint documents, you must have an appropriate viewer installed. Microsoft provides downloads of various viewers free of charge on its website, www.microsoft.com.

Printing From the CD

To print the materials for your sessions, follow these steps:

1. Insert the CD into your computer. Your computer should automatically open up a Windows Explorer window that displays a list of all files on the CD.

2. Locate the handout, PowerPoint file, tool, or support material master you are looking for and double click on the file to open it. If the file you are opening is in .pdf format, the document will open using Adobe Acrobat software. If the file you are opening uses the .ppt format, the document will open in Microsoft PowerPoint. The support material master for the evaluation forms (1 and 2) and Session-at-a-Glance tables are also offered in Microsoft Word format, so they can be personalized.

3. Print the page or pages of the document(s) that you need for the activity and session.

4. You can print the presentation slides directly from the CD using Microsoft PowerPoint. Just open the .ppt files and print as many copies as you need. You can also make handouts of the presentations by printing two, four, or six slides per page. These slides will be in color, with design elements embedded. PowerPoint also permits you to print these in grayscale or black-and-white representations. Many trainers who use personal computers to project their presentations bring along viewgraphs, just in case there are glitches in the system.

PowerPoint Presentations

The PowerPoint Slides

The PowerPoint presentation slides required for the train-the-trainer program or the topic-specific modules in chapters 5 through 10 are located on the CD as .ppt files. Each slide is double-numbered by module, according to the order in which the modules appear in the chapters. You can access individual slides by opening the PowerPoint presentations for the specific module of interest (as covered in chapters 5 through 9).

The train-the-trainer workshop uses slides to guide participants to the page they should be on and help the facilitator stay focused and manage the time.

The three-day train-the-trainer workshop uses 105 PowerPoint slides, which follow the guidelines for good PowerPoint slides and serve as a model for good training slides. They are not information dense and generally follow the 6 × 6 rule: There are no more than six words across and no more than six bullets vertically, and they use a sans-serif font.

Adapting the PowerPoint Slides

You may find it useful to modify or otherwise customize the slides by opening and editing them in the appropriate application. You must, however, retain the denotation of the original source of the material; it is illegal to pass even edited slides off as your own work. You may indicate that a document was adapted from this workbook, written and copyrighted by Elaine Biech and the American Society for Training & Development, and published by ASTD. The files will open as "Read Only," so before you adapt them, save them onto your hard drive under a different filename.

Showing the PowerPoint Slides

The following PowerPoint presentations are included on the CD:

- Module 1—Introduction (slides 1-1 through 1-11)

- Module 2—Assess and Analyze (slides 2-1 through 2-29)

- Module 3—Design and Develop (slides 3-1 through 3-30)

- Module 4—Implement and Facilitate (slides 4-1 through 4-25)

- Module 5—Evaluate and Enhance (slides 5-1 through 5-10).

The presentations are in .ppt format, which means that they will automatically show full screen when you double click on the filename. You can also open Microsoft PowerPoint and launch them from there.

Use the space bar, the enter key, or mouse clicks to advance through a presentation. Press the backspace key to back up. Use the escape key to exit a presentation. If you want to blank the screen to black as the group discusses a point, press the B key. Press it again to restore the show. If you want to blank the screen to a white background, do the same with the W key. Table A-1 summarizes these instructions.

Table A-1. Navigating Through a PowerPoint Presentation

KEY	POWERPOINT ACTION
Space bar *or* Enter *or* Mouse click	Advance through custom animations embedded in the presentation.
Backspace	Back up to the last projected element of the presentation.
Escape	Abort the presentation.
B *or* b B *or* b *(repeat)*	Blank the screen to black. Resume the presentation.
W *or* w W *or* w *(repeat)*	Blank the screen to white. Resume the presentation.

Practice with the slides before you use them to conduct a workshop. You should be able to expand on the content confidently; the Trainer's Guide (chapters 5–9) will provide additional support and information for you. If you want to engage your training participants fully (rather than worry about how to show the next slide), become familiar with this simple technology before you need to use it. One suggestion is to insert notes into the speaker's notes feature of the PowerPoint program, print them out, and have them in front of you when you present the slides.

Sessions at a Glance

The Session at a Glance is a short overview of all of the modules. It includes the list of activities (matching the activities listed in the Trainer's Guide—chapters 5 through 9—with the participant handout thumbnails in chapter 11). It also displays the amount of time an activity should take, the participant handout number, and any materials or equipment you may need. It is meant as a planning tool for you —not as an agenda for participants. You can find Session-at-a-Glance tables for all modules on the CD. From there, you may print copies to keep yourself organized during your presentation and add actual times for your session. The Session at a Glance for each module is also included in the chapter that covers that module's activities:

- Chapter 5: Module 1—Introduction

- Chapter 6: Module 2—Assess and Analyze

- Chapter 7: Module 3—Design and Develop

- Chapter 8: Module 4—Implement and Facilitate

- Chapter 9: Module 5—Evaluate and Enhance.

Handouts

These handouts are available on the CD:

Module 1: Introduction
Handout 1-1: Where's the Training Focus?
Handout 1-2: Agenda Review
Handout 1-3: What Does a Trainer Do?
Handout 1-4: What Is Training?
Handout 1-5: The Train-the-Trainer Workshop Modules
Handout 1-6: Focus on You—Wrap-Up of Module 1

Module 2: Assess and Analyze
Handout 2-1: Introduction to Module 2—Assess and Analyze
Handout 2-2: Needs Assessment and Analysis Basics
Handout 2-3: How Can You Collect Data?

Support Materials Masters

Introduction

Flipchart Preparation and List

The CD includes instructions for using flipcharts and a list of specific flipcharts to prepare.

"Team 2 Notes" Memo for Activity 2-6

During activity 2-6, you give the second team a memo, which is included on the CD. Make enough copies for approximately one-half of your class.

Pairwise Card Set for Activity 3-2

You will find a set of 22 cards on the CD. These make up 11 pairs of opposite statements. You will need one set of the cards if you have 22 participants. If you have more than 22, you will have to make extra copies, and if you have fewer than 22, you will have to remove matching statements that make up a pair. If you have an odd number of people, copy one extra statement to a pair to form one trio.

Evaluations

On the CD, you can choose from two evaluation forms (available in both PDF and Microsoft Word formats, for easy personalization). If you prefer, you could begin with one of the given evaluations and add or delete items that you want to measure.

Table Tent

The table tent should be printed on card stock and folded lengthwise. It can be in color if you print it from the CD.

Certificates

Two certificate choices appear on the CD (available in both PDF and Microsoft Word formats, for easy personalization). Select the one that best matches what is appropriate for your organization. They can be printed in color. You may want to print them on cardstock or a parchment-like paper. They are also suitable for framing.

The Masters

The following support material thumbnails can be found in full size (and some in color), for printing, on the CD.

Flipchart Preparation and List

These instructions describe the flipcharts you will need for the session. We recommend that for two teams, you have at least two flipchart stands and paper. Each team will need its own flipchart (so you may need as many as four or five) at the end of day 2 and the beginning of day 3, for the skill practice activity. Use one flipchart for pre-printed pages you have prepared before the session begins, and use the second spontaneously. We highly recommend that you purchase Mr. Sketch markers, not only for this program but for any work you do with flipcharts. They are washable, durable, and long lasting, and do not bleed through to the next page or the wall.

- Make your flipcharts more readable:
  - Write on every other page.
  - Use upper- and lowercase letters.
  - Use dark colors, no more than three colors per page.
  - Use frames, bullets, underlines, and boxes to make your flipcharts clear.
- Hang one page as a "parking lot."
- Use these flipcharts for specific modules:

MODULE 1: INTRODUCTION

Welcome
Focus Expectations (see activity 1.1)
Ground Rules (see activity 1.1)

MODULE 3: DESIGN AND DEVELOP

Learner-Focused (see activity 3.3)
Training-Focused (see activity 3.3)
Training Styles Grid (see activity 3.13)

MODULE 4: IMPLEMENT AND FACILITATE

What They Hear: What's Good? (see activity 4.5)
What They Hear: What Needs to Change? (see activity 4.5)
What They See: What's Good? (see activity 4.5)
What They See: What Needs to Change? (see activity 4.5)
Debate Timeline (see activity 4.6)
Challenges of the Profession (see activity 4.9)
Presentation Guidelines (see activities 4.10, 4.11)

"Team 2 Notes" Memo for Activity 2-6

Print enough of these memos for approximately one-half of your class.

"Team 2 Notes" Memo for Team 2 (Activity 2-6)

1. Do not reveal these instructions to the other team.
2. When the facilitator says "Start," in less than 1 minute, pass the marker around so that everyone on your team touches it without speaking.
3. The last person to touch the marker goes to the flipchart and writes:

   "Team 2—Tried and True!"

Pairwise Card Set for Activity 3-2

Copy this page and cut the 22 cards apart on the lines. Fold in half and place in a paper bag. If you have fewer than 22 participants, be sure to remove an appropriate number of cards. If you have more than 22, make extra pairs. If you have an odd number arrange so that you will have one trio.

Learner-Focused Cards	Training-Focused Cards
Trainer role is facilitator, guide, coach.	Trainer role is instructor, expert, directive.
Learning objectives are flexible.	Learning objectives are solidly established.
Learners influence pace and timing.	Trainer follows agenda.
Learn by practicing skills.	Learn by listening.
Elicit examples and ideas from participants.	Examples and ideas are all in materials.
Assume learners are experienced and knowledgeable.	Assume learners are inexperienced and have lots to learn.
Trainer asks more questions.	Trainer makes more statements.
Learners are primary resource; glean concepts from participants.	Trainer is primary resource for information, explains, and demonstrates.
Activities are primary methodology.	Lectures and discussion are primary methodology.
Learner is active participant.	Learner is passive, absorbing information.
Learning is real life and problem centered.	Learning is content centered.

Train-the-Trainer Evaluation 1

Location: _____ Date: _____

For each topic, circle two numbers. The left refers to how prepared you felt before the train-the-trainer program. The number to the right refers to how prepared you felt after the session.

1 = Unprepared   3 = Moderately Prepared   5 = Fully Prepared

Before		**After**
1 2 3 4 5	Developing correct learning objectives	1 2 3 4 5
1 2 3 4 5	Applying adult learning principles	1 2 3 4 5
1 2 3 4 5	Implementing various learning activities	1 2 3 4 5
1 2 3 4 5	Designing effective PowerPoint slides	1 2 3 4 5
1 2 3 4 5	Understanding my training style	1 2 3 4 5
1 2 3 4 5	Establishing a positive learning environment	1 2 3 4 5
1 2 3 4 5	Using effective presentation skills	1 2 3 4 5
1 2 3 4 5	Asking and answering questions	1 2 3 4 5
1 2 3 4 5	Resolving problems in the classroom	1 2 3 4 5
1 2 3 4 5	Evaluating learning	1 2 3 4 5

Use the following scale to evaluate each item:

5 = Excellent   **4 = Very Good**   **3 = Average**   **2 = Fair**   **1 = Poor**

_____ The training objectives were clearly communicated.

_____ The pace of the training was appropriate.

_____ The level of difficulty was appropriate for me.

_____ The instructor is knowledgeable about the content.

_____ The instructor answered my questions adequately.

_____ Adequate time was allowed to practice the new skills.

_____ I will apply what I learned.

What suggestions do you have to improve this train-the-trainer program?

....

....

....

....

....

Train-the-Trainer Evaluation 2

Date: _____

Use the following scale to evaluate each item:

5 = Excellent   **4 = Very Good**   **3 = Average**   **2 = Fair**   **1 = Poor**

DELIVERY

_____ Trainer delivery   _____ Trainer expertise

_____ Level of participant involvement   _____ Trainer enthusiasm

_____ Organization   _____ Trainer created a positive learning

_____ Opportunity for questions   environment

Your comments about the session:

....

....

....

....

....

CONTENT

_____ Level of subject matter   _____ Met your expectations

_____ Coverage of subject matter   _____ Transferability of ideas

What was the most valuable?

....

....

....

....

What was the least valuable?

_____

_____

_____

_____

_____

MISCELLANEOUS

_____ Quality of materials   _____ Facilities

Comments:

_____

_____

_____

_____

_____

Please provide suggestions that will help us improve this training:

_____

_____

_____

_____

_____

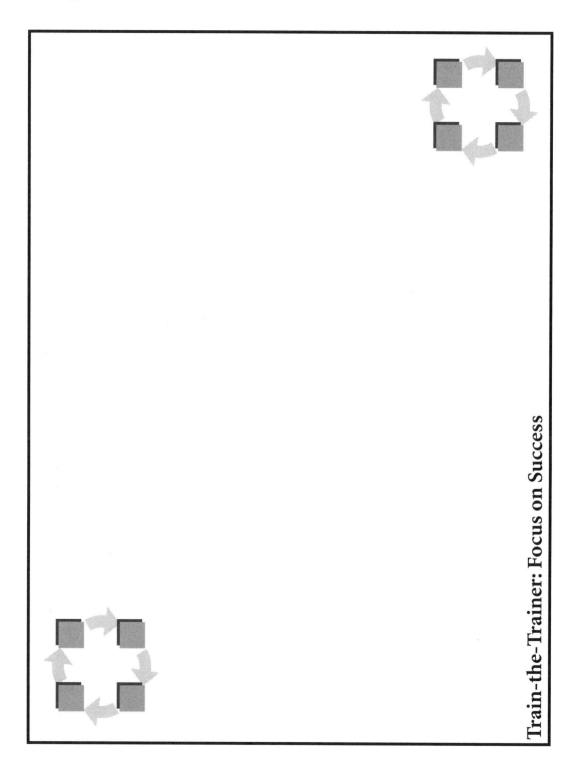

Train-the-Trainer: Focus on Success

TRAIN-THE-TRAINER CERTIFICATE

This certificate is awarded to:

[Recipient's name here]

in recognition of

Completing the Train-the-Trainer Course

Signature

Date

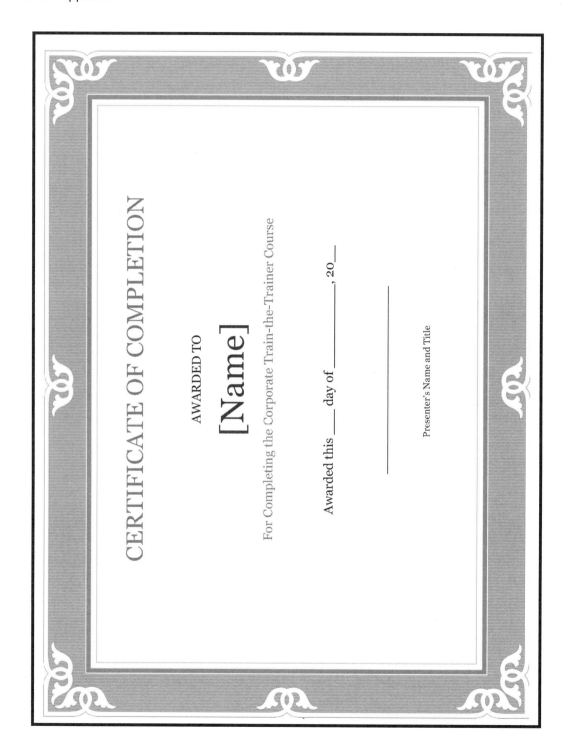

CERTIFICATE OF COMPLETION

AWARDED TO

[Name]

For Completing the Corporate Train-the-Trainer Course

Awarded this _____ day of _____, 20_____

_____
Presenter's Name and Title

Further Reading and Resources

Books
Training—General Topics

Barbazette, J. *The Art of Great Training Delivery.* San Francisco: Jossey-Bass/Pfeiffer, 2006.

Barbazette, J. *Instant Case Studies: How to Design, Adapt, and Use Case Studies in Training.* San Francisco: Jossey-Bass/Pfeiffer, 2004.

Barbazette, J. *The Trainer's Support Handbook.* New York: McGraw-Hill, 2001.

Bellman, G. *The Consultant's Calling: Bringing Who You Are to What You Do* (2nd edition). San Francisco: Jossey-Bass Publishers, 2001.

Bernthal, P., et al. ASTD *2004 Competency Study: Mapping the Future.* Alexandria, Virginia: ASTD Press, 2004.

Bersin, J. *The Blended Learning Book.* San Francisco: Jossey-Bass/Pfeiffer, 2004.

Bersin, J. *The Training Measurement Book: Best Practices, Proven Methodologies, and Practical Approaches.* San Francisco: Pfeiffer, 2008.

Biech, Elaine, editor. *ASTD Handbook for Workplace Learning Professionals.* Alexandria, Virginia: ASTD Press, 2008.

Biech, Elaine. *The Pfeiffer Book of Successful Team-Building Tools* (2nd edition). San Francisco: Jossey-Bass/Pfeiffer, 2007.

Biech, Elaine. *10 Steps to Successful Training,* Alexandria, Virginia: ASTD Press, 2009.

Biech, Elaine. *Training for Dummies.* Hoboken, New Jersey: Wiley, 2005.

Bingham, T., and T. Jeary. *Presenting Learning: Ensure CEOs Get the Value of Learning.* Alexandria, Virginia: ASTD Press, 2007.

Bossidy, L., and R. Charan. *Execution: The Discipline of Getting Things Done.* New York: Crown Business Books, 2002.

Bowman, S. *Presenting With Pizzazz.* Glenbrook, Nevada: Bowperson, 2002.

Bowman, S. *Preventing Death by Lecture.* Glenbrook, Nevada: Bowperson, 2003.

Bowman, S. *The Ten-Minute Trainer: 150 Ways to Teach It Quick and Make It Stick!* San Francisco: Pfeiffer, 2005.

Bozarth, J. *From Analysis to Evaluation: Tools, Tips, and Techniques for Trainers.* San Francisco: Pfeiffer, 2008.

Brinkerhoff, R. *Achieving Results From Training.* San Francisco: Jossey-Bass, 1999.

Broad, M., and J. Newstrom. *Transfer of Training.* New York: The Perseus Book Group, 2001.

Carliner, S. *Training Design Basics.* Alexandria, Virginia: ASTD Press, 2003.

El-Shamy, S. *How to Design and Deliver Training for the New and Emerging Generations.* San Francisco: Jossey-Bass/Pfeiffer, 2004.

Ettington, J. *The Winning Trainer* (4th edition). Woburn, Massachussetts: Butterworth-Heinemann, 2002.

Gargiulo, T., et al. *The Trainer's Portable Mentor*. San Francisco: Jossey-Bass/Pfeiffer, 2008.

Hale, J. *Performance-Based Evaluation: Tools and Techniques to Measure the Impact of Training*. San Francisco: Jossey-Bass/Pfeiffer, 2002.

Justice, T., and D. Jamieson. *The Facilitator's Fieldbook* (2nd edition). New York: AMACOM, 2006.

Kirkpatrick, D.L. *Evaluating Training Programs: The Four Levels* (3rd edition). San Francisco: Berrett-Koehler, 2006.

Knowles, M. *The Adult Learner: A Neglected Species* (3rd edition). Houston, TX: Gulf, 1984.

Knowles, M. *Self-Directed Learning*. Englewood Cliffs, New Jersey: Cambridge, 1975.

Knowles, M., et al. *The Adult Learner: The Definitive Classic in Adult Education and Human Resource Development* (5th edition). Houston: Gulf, 1998.

Kolb, D. *Learning Style Inventory*. Boston: Hay Group, 2007.

Lawson, K. *The Trainer's Handbook* (2nd edition). San Francisco: Jossey-Bass/Pfeiffer, 2006.

Lawson, K. *Train-the-Trainer: Facilitator's Guide*. San Francisco: Jossey-Bass/Pfeiffer, 1998.

Lucas, R. *The Creative Training Idea Book*. New York: AMACOM, 2003.

Mager, R. *What Every Manager Should Know About Training* (2nd edition). Atlanta: Center for Effective Performance, 1999.

McCain, D., and D. Tobey. *Facilitation Skills for Training*. Alexandria, Virginia: ASTD Press, 2007.

McCarthy, B., and J. O'Neill-Blackwell. *Hold On, You Lost Me! Use Learning Styles to Create Training That Sticks*. Alexandria, Virginia: ASTD Press, 2007.

Meier, D. *The Accelerated Learning Handbook: A Creative Guide to Designing and Delivering Faster, More Effective Training Programs*. New York: McGraw Hill, 2002.

Millbower, L. *Showbiz Training*. New York: AMACON, 2003.

Phillips, J. *Return on Investment in Training and Performance Improvement Programs*. Alexandria, Virginia: ASTD Press, 1997.

Phillips, J., and P. Phillips. *Beyond Learning Objectives: Develop Measurable Objectives That Link to the Bottom Line*. ASTD Press, 2008.

Phillips, J., and P. Phillips. *ROI at Work*. Alexandria, Virginia: ASTD Press, 2005.

Phillips, J., and P. Phillips. *ROI in Action*. San Francisco: Jossey-Bass/Pfeiffer, 2008.

Phillips, J., and P. Phillips. *Show Me the Money: How to Determine ROI in People, Projects, and Programs*. San Francisco: Berrett-Koehler, 2007.

Pike, R. *One-on-One Training: How to Effectively Train One Person at a Time*. San Francisco: Jossey-Bass/Pfeiffer, and Creative Training Techniques Press, 2000.

Pike, R. *Creative Training Techniques Handbook* (3rd edition). Amherst, Massachusetts: HRD Press, 2003.

Piskurich, G., ed. *The ASTD Handbook of Training and Delivery*. New York: McGraw-Hill, 1999.

Piskurich, G. *Rapid Instructional Design*. San Francisco: John Wiley, 2000.

Piskurich, G. *Trainer Basics*. Alexandria, Virginia: ASTD Press, 2003.

Robinson, D., and J. Robinson. *Performance Consulting: A Practical Guide for HR and Learning Professionals* (2nd edition). San Francisco: Berrett-Koehler, 2008.

Robinson, D., and J. Robinson. *Moving From Training to Performance*. San Francisco: Berrett-Koehler, 1998.

Rosania, R. *Presentation Basics*. Alexandria, Virginia: ASTD Press, 2003.

Rossett, A. *First Things Fast: A Handbook for Performance Analysis*. San Francisco: Jossey-Bass/Pfeiffer, 1997.

Rothwell, W., and H.C. Kazanas. *Improving on-the-Job Training: How to Establish and Operate a Comprehensive OJT Program* (2nd edition). San Francisco: Jossey-Bass/Pfeiffer, 2004.

Rothwell, W., and H.C. Kazanas. *Mastering the Instructional Design Process* (3rd edition). San Francisco: Jossey-Bass/Pfeiffer, 2004.

Russell, L. *Training Triage: Performance-Based Solutions Amid Chaos, Confusion, and Change.* Alexandria, Virginia: ASTD Press, 2005.

Silberman, M. *Active Training* (2nd edition). San Francisco: Jossey-Bass/Pfeiffer, 1998.

Silberman, M. *The Handbook of Experiential Learning.* San Francisco: Pfeiffer, 2007.

Silberman, M., ed. *The 2006 ASTD Training and Performance Sourcebook.* Alexandria, Virginia: ASTD Press, 2006.

Stolovitch, H., and E. Keeps. *Telling Ain't Training,* Alexandria, Virginia: ASTD Press, 2002.

Tamblyn, D. *Laugh and Learn.* New York: AMACOM, 2003.

Thiagarajan, S. *Design Your Own Games and Activities.* San Francisco: Jossey-Bass/Pfeiffer, 2003.

Ukens, L. *All Together Now! A Seriously Fun Collection of Interactive Training Games and Activities.* San Francisco: Jossey-Bass/Pfeiffer, 2008.

Ukens, L. *What Smart Trainers Know: The Secrets of Success From the World's Foremost Experts.* San Francisco: Jossey-Bass/Pfeiffer, 2001.

Wick C., et al. *The Six Disciplines of Breakthrough Learning: How to Turn Training and Development Into Business Results,* San Francisco: Pfeiffer, 2006.

Activities, Games, and Surveys

Barca, M., and Cobb, K. *Beginnings & Endings.* Amherst, Massachusetts: HRD Press, 1993.

Biech, Elaine. *90 World-Class Activities by 90 World-Class Trainers.* San Francisco: Pfeiffer, 2007.

Biech, Elaine, editor. *The Pfeiffer Annual: Training.* San Francisco: Jossey-Bass/Pfeiffer, 1972–2010.

Biech, Elaine. *Trainer's Warehouse Book of Games: Fun and Energizing Ways to Enhance Learning.* San Francisco: Pfeiffer, 2008.

Burn, B. *Assessments A to Z: A Collection of 50 Questionnaires, Instruments, and Inventories.* San Francisco: Jossey-Bass/Pfeiffer, 2000.

Carosilli, M. *Great Session Openers, Closers, and Energizers.* New York: McGraw-Hill, 1998.

Gordon. *Pfeiffer's Classic Inventories, Questionnaires, and Surveys for Training and Development.* Jossey-Bass/Pfeiffer, 2004.

Kapp, K. *Gadgets, Games and Gizmos for Learning: Tools and Techniques for Transferring Know-How From Boomers to Gamers.* San Francisco: Pfeiffer, 2007.

McLaughlin, M., and S. Peyser. *The New Encyclopedia of Icebreakers.* San Francisco: Jossey-Bass/Pfeiffer, 2004.

Pike, B., and L. Solem. *50 Creative Training Openers and Energizers.* San Francisco: Jossey-Bass/Pfeiffer, 2000.

Scannell, E.E., and J. Newstrom. *The Big Book of Presentation Games.* New York: McGraw-Hill, 1998.

Scannell, E.E., and J. Newstrom. *Games Trainers Play Series.* New York: McGraw-Hill, 1983–1998.

Silberman, M. *The Best of Active Training: 25 One-Day Workshops.* San Francisco: Jossey-Bass/Pfeiffer, 2004.

Sugar, S., and J. Whitcomb. *Training Games: Simple and Effective Techniques to Engage and Motivate Learners.* Alexandria, Virginia: ASTD Press, 2006.

Tamblyn, D., and S. Weiss. *The Big Book of Humorous Training Games.* McGraw-Hill, New York 2000.

Thiagarajan, S. *Thiagi's Interactive Lectures: Power Up Your Training With Interactive Games and Exercises*. Alexandria, Virginia: ASTD Press, 2005.

Thiagarajan, S. *Card Games by Thiagi: A User's Guide*. Alexandria, Virginia: ASTD Press, 2007.

Thiagarajan, S. *Thiagi's 100 Favorite Games*. San Francisco: Pfeiffer, 2006.

Ukens, L. *Energize Your Audience: 75 Quick Activities That Get Them Started and Keep Them Going*. San Francisco: Jossey-Bass/Pfeiffer, 2000.

Ukens, L. *The New Encyclopedia of Group Activities*. San Francisco: Jossey-Bass/Pfeiffer, 2004.

VanGundy, A. *101 Great Games and Activities*. San Francisco: Jossey-Bass/Pfeiffer, 1998.

West, E. *201 Icebreakers*. New York: McGraw-Hill, 1997.

Creativity and the Brain

Biech, Elaine. *The ASTD Trainer's Sourcebook, Creativity, and Innovation*. New York: McGraw-Hill, 1996.

Cameron, J. *The Artist's Way: A Spiritual Path to Higher Creativity*. New York: Putnam, 1992.

Herrmann, Ned. *The Creative Brain*. Lake Lure, North Carolina: The Ned Herrmann Group, 1995.

Lucas, R.W. *Creative Learning: Activities and Games that REALLY Engage People*. San Francisco: Pfeiffer, 2007.

Lucas, R.W. *The Creative Training Idea Book: Inspired Tips and Techniques for Engaging and Effective Learning*. New York: AMACOM, 2003.

Millbower, L. *Training With a Beat: The Teaching Power of Music*. Sterling, Virginia: Stylus, 2000.

Von Oech, R. *A Whack on the Side of the Head* (3rd edition). New York: Warner, 1998.

E-learning

Arch, D., and S. Ensz. *Web-Based Interactive Learning Activities*. Amherst, Massachusetts: Recommended Resources, 2000.

Aldrich, C. *Simulations and the Future of Learning: An Innovative (and Perhaps Revolutionary) Approach to e-Learning*. San Francisco: Jossey-Bass/Pfeiffer, 2004.

Allen, M. *Creating Successful e-Learning: A Rapid System for Getting It Right First Time, Every Time*. San Francisco: Pfeiffer, 2006.

Allen, M. *e-learning Annual*. San Francisco: Pfeiffer, 2008.

Carliner, S. *Designing e-Learning*. Alexandria, Virginia: ASTD Press, 2002.

Clark, R. *e-Learning and the Science of Instruction: Proven Guidelines for Consumers and Designers of Multimedia Learning*. San Francisco: Jossey-Bass/Pfeiffer, 2003.

Clark, R.C. *Developing Technical Training: A Structured Approach for Developing Classroom and Computer-Based Instructional Materials*. San Francisco: Pfeiffer, 2007.

Driscoll, M. *Web-Based Training: Creating e-learning Experiences* (2nd edition). San Francisco: Jossey-Bass/Pfeiffer, 2002.

Hofmann, J. *Live and Online!* (with CD-ROM). San Francisco: Jossey-Bass/Pfeiffer, 2004.

Islam, K. *Podcasting 101 for Training and Development: Challenges, Opportunities, and Solutions*. San Francisco: Pfeiffer, 2008.

Lee, W., and D. Owens. *Multimedia-Based Instructional Design*. San Francisco: Jossey-Bass/Pfeiffer, 2004.

Piskurich, G. *Preparing Learners for e-Learning*. San Francisco: Jossey-Bass/Pfeiffer, 2003.

Piskurich, G. *Getting the Most From Online Learning.* San Francisco: Jossey-Bass/Pfeiffer, 2004.

Shank, P., and A. Sitze. *Making Sense of Online Learning: A Guide for the Beginners and the Truly Skeptical.* San Francisco: Jossey-Bass/Pfeiffer, 2004.

Graphics and Design

Arch, D., and I. Torgrimson, *Flipchart Magic.* Amherst, Massachusetts: HRD Press, 1999.

Brandt, R. *Flipcharts.* San Francisco: Jossey-Bass/Pfeiffer, 1997.

Lucas, R.W. *The Big Book of Flipcharts.* New York: McGraw-Hill, 1999.

Millbower, L. *Cartoons for Trainers.* Sterling, Virginia: Stylus, 2002.

Sonneman, M. *Beyond Words: A Guide to Drawing Ideas.* Berkeley: Ten Speed Press, 1997.

Monthly Publications

ASTD *Infoline*
American Society for Training & Development
1640 King Street, P.O. Box 1443, Alexandria, VA 22313
www.astd.org

T+D
American Society for Training & Development
1640 King Street, P.O. Box 1443, Alexandria, VA 22313
www.astd.org

Training Magazine
Nielsen Business Media
770 Broadway, New York, NY 10003
www.trainingmag.com

Products

Assessment Instruments, Simulations, and Games

HRD Press
22 Amherst Road
Amherst, MA 01002
(800) 822-2801 www.hrdpress.com

HRDQ
2002 Renaissance Boulevard #100
King of Prussia, PA 19406
(610) 292-2614 www.hrdq.com

Human Synergistics
39819 Plymouth Road
Plymouth, MI 48170
(313) 459-1030 www.humansynergistics.com

Pfeiffer/Jossey-Bass
989 Market Street
San Francisco, CA 94103
(800) 274-4434 www.pfeiffer.com

Clip Art

Click Art, PrintMaster, Print Shop
Broderbund
88 Rowland Way
Novato, CA 94945
(415) 895-2000 www.broderbund.com

COSMI
2600 Homestead Place
Rancho Dominguez, CA 90220
(310) 886-3510 www.cosmi.com

Jupiterimages
5232 E. Pima Street
Suite 200C
Tucson, AZ 85712
1-800-482-4567 www.clipart.com

Key Click Art
The Learning Company
One Athenaeum Street
Cambridge, MA 02142
(800) 845-8692 www.learningco.com

Creative Training Products

Bob Pike Group
7620 West 78th Street
 Minneapolis, MN 55439-2518
(800) 383-9210 www.bobpikegroup.com

Creative Presentation Resources, Inc.
P.O. Box 180487
Casselberry, FL 32718-0487
(407) 695-5535 (800) 308-0399 www.presentationresources.net

Trainer's Warehouse
89 Washington Avenue
Natick, MA 01760
(508) 653-3770 (800) 299-3770 www.trainerswarehouse.com

Graphic Art Materials

Chartpak
(800) 788-5572 www.chartpak.com

Staedtler, Inc.
P.O. Box 2196
Chatsworth, CA 91311
(800) 776-5544 www.staedtler-USA.com

Music

Classical Archives, LLC
200 Sheridan Avenue, Suite 403
Palo Alto, CA 94306
(650) 330-8050 www.classicalarchives.com

The Music Bakery
7522 Campbell Road, #133-2
Dallas, TX 75248
(800) 229-0313 www.musicbakery.com

Network Music, LLC
15150 Avenue of Science
San Diego, CA 92128
(858) 451-6400 www.networkmusic.com

Offbeat Training®
(407) 256-0501 www.offbeattraining.com

Paper Supplies

Baudville
5380 52nd Street, S.E.
Grand Rapids, MI 49512-9765
(800) 728-0888 www.baudville.com

Idea Art
P.O. Box 291505
Nashville, TN 37229-1505
(800) 435-2278 www.ideaart.com

Paper Direct
P.O. Box 2970
Colorado Springs, CO 80901-2970
(800) 272-7377 www.paperdirect.com

Presentation Equipment and Accessories

Clearanswer Limited
11604 Carlsbad Road
Reno, NV 89506
(775) 845-7626 www.clearanswer.com

Graphic Products
P.O. Box 4030
Beaverton, OR 97076-4030
(800) 788-5572 www.graphicproducts.com

Neuland North America Ltd.
P.O. Box 6745
Great Falls, MT 59406-6745
(888) 713-2333 www.neuland.biz

Props, Toys, and Training Tools

Creative Learning Tools
P.O. Box 37
Wausau, WI 54402
(715) 842-2467 www.creativelearningtools.com

M&N International
P.O. Box 64784
St. Paul, MN 55164-0784
(800) 479-2043 www.mninternational.com

Oriental Trading Company
P.O. Box 2659
Omaha, NE 68103-2659
(800) 526-9300 www.orientaltrading.com

Trainers Warehouse
89 Washington Avenue
Natick, MA 01760
(800) 299-3770 www.trainerswarehouse.com

Videos and Films

American Media Inc.
4900 University Avenue
West Des Moines, IA 50266-6769
(800) 262-2557 www.americanmediainc.com

CRM Films
2215 Faraday Avenue
Carlsbad, CA 92008-7295
(800) 421-0833 www.crmlearning.com

Licensing

American Society of Composers, Authors and Publishers (ASCAP)
Music
One Lincoln Plaza
New York, NY 10023
(800) 952-7227 www.ascap.com

Broadcasting Music, Inc (BMI)
Music
10 Music Square East
Nashville, TN 32703
(800) 925-8451 www.bmi.com

Copyright Clearance Center, Inc.
photos, electronics, books, newsletters, magazines, newspapers
222 Rosewood Drive
Danvers, MA 01923
(978) 750-8400 www.copyright.com

About the Author

Elaine Biech is president and managing principal of ebb associates inc, an organization development firm that helps organizations work through large-scale change. She has been in the training and consulting field for 30 years, and she works with business, government, and nonprofit organizations.

Elaine specializes in helping people work as teams to maximize their effectiveness. Customizing all of her work for individual clients, she conducts strategic planning sessions and implements corporate-wide systems, such as quality improvement, reengineering of business processes, and mentoring programs. Elaine facilitates topics such as coaching today's employee, fostering creativity, customer service, time management, stress management, speaking skills, training competence, conducting productive meetings, managing change, handling the difficult employee, organizational communication, conflict resolution, and effective listening.

Known as the trainer's trainer, Elaine has developed media presentations and training materials and has presented at dozens of national and international conferences. Elaine designs custom training programs for managers, leaders, trainers, and consultants, and her work has been featured in dozens of publications, including *The Wall Street Journal, Harvard Management Update, The Washington Post,* and *Fortune* magazine.

As a management and executive consultant, trainer, and designer, Elaine has provided services to FAA, Land O' Lakes, McDonald's, Lands' End, General Casualty Insurance, Chrysler, Johnson Wax, PricewaterhouseCoopers, American Family Insurance, Marathon Oil, Hershey Chocolate, Federal Reserve Bank, the U.S. Navy, NASA, Newport News Shipbuilding, Kohler Company, ASTD, American Red Cross, Association of Independent Certified Public Accountants, the University of Wisconsin, the College of William and Mary, ODU, and hundreds of other public and private sector organizations, to prepare them for the challenges of the new millennium.

In addition, Elaine is the author and editor of more than four dozen books and articles, including, *10 Steps to Successful Training,* 2009; *The Consultant's Quick Start Guide,* 2nd ed., 2009; *ASTD Handbook for Workplace Learning Professionals,* 2008; *Trainer's Warehouse Book of Games,* 2008; *The Business of Consulting,* 2nd ed., 2007; *Thriving Through Change*: *A Leader's Practical Guide to Change Mastery,* 2007;

Successful Team-Building Tools, 2nd ed., 2007; *90 World-Class Activities by 90 World-Class Trainers*, 2007 (named a Training Review Best Training Product of 2007); nine-volume set of *ASTD's Certification Study Guides*, 2006; *12 Habits of Successful Trainers*, ASTD Infoline, 2005; *The ASTD Infoline Dictionary of Basic Trainer Terms*, 2005; *Training for Dummies*, 2005; *Marketing Your Consulting Services*, 2003; *The Consultant's Quick Start Guide*, 2001; *The Consultant's Legal Guide*, 2000; *Interpersonal Skills: Understanding Your Impact on Others*, 1996; *Building High Performance*, 1998; *The Pfeiffer Annual for Consultants* and *The Pfeiffer Annual for Trainers* (1998–2010); *The ASTD Sourcebook: Creativity and Innovation—Widen Your Spectrum*, 1996; *The HR Handbook*, 1996; *Ten Mistakes CEOs Make About Training*, 1995; *TQM for Training*, 1994; *Diagnostic Tools for Total Quality*, INFO-LINE, 1991; *Managing Teamwork*, 1994; *Process Improvement: Achieving Quality Together*, 1994; *Business Communications*, 1992; *Delegating for Results*, 1992; *Increased Productivity Through Effective Meetings*, 1987; and *Stress Management: Building Healthy Families*, 1984. Her books have been translated into Chinese, German, and Dutch.

Elaine received her BS from the University of Wisconsin–Superior in Business and Education Consulting and received her MS in Human Resource Development from the University of Wisconsin–Superior. Active at the national level of ASTD, Elaine is a lifetime member, served on the 1990 National Conference Design Committee, was a member of the National ASTD Board of Directors and Secretary of ASTD from 1991 to 1994, initiated and chaired Consultant's Day for seven years, and was the International Conference Design Chair in 2000. In addition to her work with ASTD, she has served on the Independent Consultants Association's (ICA) Advisory Committee and on the Instructional Systems Association (ISA) board of directors.

In 2001, Elaine received ISA's highest award, The ISA Spirit Award. She is also the recipient of the 1992 National ASTD Torch Award, the 2004 ASTD Volunteer-Staff Partnership Award, and the 2006 ASTD Gordon M. Bliss Memorial Award. In addition, she was selected for the 1995 Wisconsin Women Entrepreneur's Mentor Award. For the past 12 years, Elaine has been the consulting editor for the prestigious *Training and Consulting Annuals*, published by Jossey-Bass/Pfeiffer.

Index